Faint praise for *T*

"Whoever said truth is stranger than fiction never read one of Taylor's books…Unjustly remorseful and anything but witty."
—*Moosejaw Gazette*

"A splashy attempt." —*Field & Stream*

"I don't know, I like, learned some stuff." —*Jerome K. Sphincter*

"Dangerous? Wicked? Forbidden? You bet…pour yourself a bucket of chips and dig in." —*Mayhem County Times*

Really comic, really tragic, bracingly unsentimental…Total trash! Complete nonsense!" —*Newport News*

"A rollicking good read that, as the Irish say, would make a dead man laugh." —*Philadelphia Inquirer*

"Taylor has really stepped in it this time, and left footprints all over the place." —*Downe Township Picayune*

"If I had a dime for every amusing thing Taylor has written, I'd have forty cents. Which is the same number of books he's written. A farce."
—*The Pagan Press*

"The term Bestseller simply does not apply here. Badsmeller would be more appropriate." —*Confusion Today*

The Book of Wedges

Tales from a Beach

Hal Taylor

WITH A FORWARD BY THE AUTHOR

TO ROSG MARY — WITH ALL BEST WISHES!

Hal Tay 11/21

Library of Congress Control Number: 2021908636

ISBN: 978-1-7923-6762-5

Book, cover designs, and illustrations are
by the author unless otherwise stated.

The text is set in Minion Pro

The historical information presented in this book
concerning wedges, as well as regional
Delaware Valley history, can easily be referenced by
searching online.

To see more of Hal Taylor's work visit:
www.haltaylorillustration.com

The following people contributed to this book in one way or another. Many are not even aware they did. And some have gone to an even better beach.

Bill Shea (New Guy), Helen Shea (New Girl), Will Shea, Pete Wagner, Tommy T., Drew and Susan Tibbets (parents of Bear and Max), Ben, Kathy, and Annie Curtis, Art, Worm, Gary & Claudia, Marie & Perry, Jake & Edie, Fisherman Joe & Rita, Trader Joe, Broadway Joe, Lobster Man, Mr. Munson, Roger & Gale, Jean Lewis & John Sockwell, Mama Lew, Clayton West, Rick Hoey, Carol Duffy, Tom Duffy, Lenny Large, Myron & Judy, Charlie, the other Charlie, Milo & Otis, Meghan Wren, Harry and Linda Van Norman, Jack & Lorraine DiLaurentis, Linda Hampton, Janet Moretti, Michael Youngkin, Marlee Herman, Andrew S. Lewis.

Special thanks to my editor, Jennifer (Hawkeye) Boone, and of course, Painter John Gilligan.

Contents

FORWARD

or this, my latest effort, I was hoping to find someone notable to write a forward for it. But since my name is not on the tip of everyone's tongue in the literary-world, or few other places, for that matter, I was unable to attract anyone willing to attach their name to it. So I thought I would turn to an old acquaintance for the task, someone who knows me intimately: Harald of Haddon. It was an enormous mistake.

We first ran head-on into each other, many, many years ago in a run-down shell of a city that slumps on the banks of the Delaware River. Like Harald, its best days are far behind it. It was once thriving, unlike Harald who has never been accused of doing anything productive. Real work is something he has never been a party to.

With one foot in the Middle Ages and the other foot in his mouth, he materializes occasionally seemingly out of nowhere, looking like he just escaped from a fight with a raccoon over the contents of a dumpster, and the raccoon won. But he still maintains an air of defiance with his wing-tip poulaines, filthy knickers, a cloak smeared with ancient gravy stains, and either a caved-in bowler hat or baseball cap with frayed fabric hanging from the brim like cobwebs.

He will whine and grouse about how he spends a large portion of his day at the greengrocer's trying to pry apart plastic bags that seem to be welded together, the difficulty of trying to spread peanut butter on top of jelly, how band-aid packaging is nearly impossible to open while you are bleeding to death from a paper cut, or why he has to pay for TV movies that he wants to see, while the ones he doesn't want are free. When the ranting finally tapers off, he asks for money, I refuse, and he stumbles back into the ether the same way he arrived.

Harald claims direct ties to England by way of the town of Haddonfield, New Jersey. It was founded by Elizabeth Haddon, who arrived in West Jersey from Southwark, London in 1701. The land that it occupies was purchased from William Penn by Elizabeth's father, John Haddon.

However, unable to make the journey to take possession of the acquisition due to poor health, he sent his young daughter instead. She named the eventual town for him, which for many years has been considered one of the tonier hamlets in South Jersey.

Since Harald's father was a resident of Haddonfield, he feels it gives him an indelible link to-old world sophistication, hence his self-styled moniker. To add more credibility, his father later purchased a home in Haddon Heights, NJ, also linked to the Haddon family. Coincidentally, that is exactly my father's history as well.

I detest resorting to the overused term "evil twin", but I'm afraid it may be appropriate in this case. Our lives have been inextricably entwined since birth. Maybe there is something about this astrology business after all since we're both Geminis. But we are as dissimilar as if we came from different species. Curiously though, when asked how he's doing, Harald often remarks, "If I were any better, there would have to be two of me." He knows something.

He was once reprimanded in grade school for concocting tall tales. For a show and tell event, he sat in front of the class and unraveled a completely fictitious narrative about how his parents were deep-sea divers, who traveled around the world exploring, and how he was also a diver who had his very own pet octopus. The teacher sent a letter home to his parents letting them know about their son's vivid imagination. He intercepted the letter and disposed of it. After a brief period of time his mind gravitated to other things and the fairy tales took a back seat. His teacher thought he had made progress and added a note to his report card stating that Harald had "finally come back down to earth." His mother had no idea what it meant and confronted him about it, whereas he merely shrugged and pleaded ignorance. Incidentally, I have also been known to invent a story or two. You may be wondering at this point if we might be the same person but, as you can see, there are so few similarities that I will not insult your intelligence by implying such a thing. We'll just leave it there.

Despite serious misgivings, I asked Harald to write the forward for *The Book of Wedges*. He gleefully agreed, although there was a strange gleam in his eye. He then disappeared and for months afterward I heard nothing from him. Then one gloomy, winter day he presented me with his effort and snickered.

Knowing Haddon as I did, I did not expect a glowing tribute, but I supposed he would render something faintly complimentary. I was totally unprepared for what I encountered: a complete character assassination. Here's an excerpt from his hatchet job:

What is not clear when first meeting Taylor, but becomes obvious after just a short time, is his total lack of talent...and shame. He has never found anyone as fascinating as himself. He will prattle on about his many accomplishments, almost all of which are complete fabrications. He was born that way. I, on the other hand, am level-headed, charming, and can walk in a straight line, usually.

And now, I am sorry to say, he has done more serious damage. Having read this latest travesty, I must condemn it as empty and meaningless dribble. Truly, it echoes the very psyche of the man himself. It is cheap, crass, and deeply flawed.

And where do I begin critiquing the alleged illustrations? I have seen far better art created by toddlers that have been attached to refrigerator doors by their grandparents. He is a hack, nothing more. What is worse is that despite his exhaustive self-interest, he pretends to be humble, but to borrow a phrase from my fellow countryman Winston Churchill, "He has much to be humble about."

However, I begrudgingly take pity on this pathetic and inept individual as he is approaching the time of life when he is simply old and in the way. Plus, he begged me to say a few good words on his behalf. And he paid me.

Haddon's painful diatribe proves the old aphorism that if you want something done right, do it yourself. And thus concludes the self-authored forward to my own book.

So now that you know what you're dealing with, read on at your own peril. But be forewarned, the contents may cause internal bleeding, hypothermia, kilts, ear lobes, bed sores, or worse.

(Credit cards, personal checks, PayPal, Venmo, cash, and any other forms of legal tender are gladly accepted.)

HAL TAYLOR

IT DON'T RAIN ON GOOD PEOPLE.

—*Jake Green*

In the Beginning

he waters of the Delaware River flow over 300 miles before they lap the shoreline of a spit of sand on the Delaware Bay known as Gandy's Beach. It was at this little beach front community that my wife and I rented a house, a shack actually, for several years in the 1990s.

Gandy's Beach is part of what is referred to as The Bayshore, a forty-mile stretch of New Jersey's portion of the Delaware River estuary. The region was once prosperous but has been in a downturn since the 1950's when its prime revenue producer, the oyster industry, was devastated by a parasitic disease.

About a mile in length, Gandy's Beach is bound on the north end by Nantuxent Cove, and at its south end by a marina which was effectively put out of business by Hurricane Sandy. A number of other properties were severely damaged by the storm as well, including the home of a friend that was completely washed away. Fortunately, he had a spare home, also at Gandy's. There are presently about sixty houses still standing, most of them much more opulent than the place we used to occupy.

Hurricane Sandy was not Gandy's first storm. A devastating flood in 1950 ripped houses from their moorings and scattered them throughout the nearby marsh. Similar carnage was unleashed in 1980 during a powerful nor'easter.

All that remained of the ruined homes were old pilings and concrete septic tanks half-buried in the sand of the beach. Our kids used to crawl in and out and on top of them. That was their playground.

Septic tanks are still very much in use at Gandy's Beach. There is no sewer service. There is no water service either; all the properties are connected to wells. There are electricity and telephone lines but no trash collection; it's up to the residents to haul their garbage and recyclables to the Downe Township Convenience Center, open on Wednesdays and Saturdays.

This is precisely the type of situation that breeds opportunity. On Sunday afternoons, we used to look forward to a visit from "Can Man", a wizened old fossil who would slowly drive down Cove Road in an ancient station wagon and pick up the weekend collection of empty cans and bottles to resell. Appearing to be in his seventies, he was always shirtless, his wrinkled skin the color of a walnut. His collection technique was simplicity itself. He would merely toss the cans and bottles into the back of the station wagon: no barrels, buckets, or bags to separate glass from aluminum. The aroma preceded him.

Can Man never shied away from conversation; he always had some complaint to share with us. Often, it was about his alleged young girlfriend who he claimed was stealing his money, or he would describe his fist fight with another can man who worked Fortescue and was trying to steal his business. He would enthusiastically show us the scar from his latest operation. We, of course, did our part to contribute to Can Man's livelihood.

The kitchen is the soul of any home, especially so at a beach house. The stove and refrigerator are the heart and stomach, and they need to be in good working order. Ours were not. In fact, both died around the same time. I have previously described the state of both of these kitchen necessities in my first book, *The Illustrated Delaware River: The History of a Great American River.* While Gandy's Beach is not exactly on another planet, it is just far enough off the beaten path that appliance repair was difficult to summon. It was time for new kitchen essentials. But due to budgetary restraints, we would have to settle for previously owned or, to use the current term, "gently used" equipment.

We were able to procure a used fridge so we could continue to babysit the canned ham which had been left by the owners, who occasionally reminded us not to throw it out. My brother-in-law John had a pickup truck and offered to help me take the old fridge to the Convenience Center. With great effort, we managed to manhandle it out of the house and into the back of the truck. Off we drove through the marsh where a huge flock of snow geese were grazing to bulk up for their return trip to the Arctic.

We arrived at the convenience center only to be informed that they do not accept appliances. Time for a change in plans. We spent the rest of the day trying to figure out what to do with it. Finally, John was able

Gandy's Beach, Cove Road. The good old days.

to contact a charity that would take it for a homeless shelter. Another problem for people who already had problems.

We also bought a used stove and contacted a junk dealer from Trenton who showed up one Friday afternoon to haul the old one away. When the junk man arrived, he wanted to know if this was the right place. He was genuinely terrified to be so close to such a large body of water, constantly looking over his shoulder as if he expected a sudden tidal wave.

We helped him wrestle the stove out of the house while his assistant stood watching. The assistant was a small skinny guy who wore an old buckskin coat that was two sizes too big for him. I have never seen it's equal before or since. It was an unusual light tan color and was so worn that it had a patina that can only be described as looking like the an-

A T-shirt design I did in the 90s. It was not a big success.
The few shirts that still exist are used to mop up nasty spills.

cient calfskin vellum that was used for the *Book of Kells*. It was actually luminescent.

The stove was loaded onto the small trailer the junk man had brought along with other refuse to be carted off to who knows where. He was extremely relieved to finally be leaving the beach. Nervously lighting a cigarette, he said he couldn't understand how people could live here next to all that water.

THE EVER-POPULAR BEACH GLASS, or sea glass, can be found just about anywhere in the world where there is a beach. The pieces can be polished from their natural frosty surface to a sparkling jewel-like quality. It washes up from broken bottles, tableware, and other glass detritus lost in the seven seas and tumbled and tossed over many years to varying degrees of smoothness. But Gandy's Beach had it delivered.

When we were first introduced to the beach and its residents, we couldn't help but notice that every home seemed to have a collection of the same bluish-green-colored pieces of glass, ranging from small shards to chunks weighing as much as ten pounds. They lined bookshelves, fruit bowls, and the bottoms of fish tanks.

Gandy's is about eleven miles south of Millville, NJ, the home of Wheaton Glass, which began in 1888 as a manufacturer of pharmaceutical glass. South Jersey is ideally suited to the glass industry due to an abundance of natural resources needed to make it: wood, sand, soda ash, and silica. Wheaton became quite a huge company, producing vast amounts of products and with it, waste. The story, as I heard it from local sources, is that Wheaton hauled broken glass and slag to Gandy's and simply unloaded it on the beach. Some of the larger pieces actually looked like rocks.

So not only was the beach littered with debris from storm-ravaged homes and discarded glass, but also with surplus construction materials

Wallace the Wetlands

piled along sections of the beach from futile attempts to stem erosion. Some folks might say the place was a dump, and they would be correct. But it was our dump.

THE REST OF THE ENVIRONMENT, however, was anything but dumpy. The only access to Gandy's was a two-lane road that snaked through the wetlands; a vast network of creeks and streams coursing through acres upon acres of salt marsh that divided solid ground from the bay. It was covered in native grasses like Carex, Japanese Stiltgrass, Marshmallow, and

Spartina patens, also known as salt hay, commercially harvested on the Bayshore for some 200 years. Native cattails, however, were rapidly being replaced by invasive Phragmites. All these grasses displayed a constantly changing palette composed of pale green in the spring, rich greens in the summer, fading to burnt ochre in the fall, and pale straw in the winter.

The marsh was also home to muskrats, great blue herons, great white herons, great egrets, lesser egrets, mud hens, ducks, geese, gulls, terns, and countless other shore birds. Untold varieties of fish, eels, blue crabs, horse-shoe crabs, fiddler crabs and other sea creatures used the environment as a nursery. It was wild, desolate, majestic, and stunningly beautiful. When we crossed the meadows on our way to the beach, it was a barrier that shut out the rest of the world that said, "Don't call us, we'll call you."

▸ ▸ ▸

THE HOUSE NEXT TO OURS at Gandy's Beach was owned by a gentleman known to everyone as Painter John, as lovable a human being as ever lived. He came by that name not because he was an artist or a professional painter, but because of an incident that occurred when he should have been doing one thing, but wound up doing another. More about that later.

Painter John was both simple and complex, naive and worldly. He was an outdoorsman, enjoyed hunting nearly as much as fishing and owned several hunting dogs that he took out occasionally. He never brought the hunting dogs to the beach, though; that was reserved for his house dog, a precocious little Shih Tzu named "Sweepers". On one hunting trip, he and the dogs got themselves turned around in a wood-ed area and became lost. After traipsing around for quite a while they finally came to the edge of civilization and found a 7-11. John went in to get some bottled water for his thirsty dogs but complained bitterly afterward that they didn't have the cheap stuff and he was forced to buy "Pierre Water."

I was once witness to a lively discussion in the front room of our house between Painter John and another neighbor named Tommy T. over what is now a long-forgotten topic. The rhythm of the conversation flowed genially back and forth but gradually began to increase in intensity as the two participants became more and more divided over their opinions. Voices raised, hands gesticulated, fists pounded, and beer was spilled, but neither man refused to give sway to the other's point of view. Finally, as the dispute reached its apex, Tommy said "John, you don't know what you're talking about." But Painter John, having run out of retorts, claimed victory by citing what could have passed for long-lost holy scripture: "Tom…it's right in **THE BOOK OF WEDGES!**"

To Painter John, The Book of Wedges was the standard for everything; it removed all doubt.

A statement that resounding cannot be forgotten. It's as eye-opening as seeing the floor of your favorite bar in broad daylight. Now, many years after the fact, this is the Gospel according to Painter John.

There are indeed wedges involved…a wedge-shaped parcel of unclaimed land left over from the Mason-Dixon survey; a dreaded situation in the already infuriating game of golf; an ancient form of writing; the origin of a certain style of women's shoes; pie charts; rock splitting, and a pottery technique.

Alternating with the many aspects of wedges, are tales from the inimitable Painter John and of Gandy's Beach itself, some of which may actually contain a kernel of truth: a disappointing encounter with a tall ship, a disappearing sign, the joy of crabs, and the quest for lima beans.

It's an intimate glimpse into a more innocent time that is presented here as it was: a crappy little shack on pilings with bad plumbing, no phone, no TV, no Internet, no air conditioning. Just ourselves, kids, family, and friends, as it is written in…

The Book of Wedges

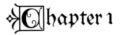hapter 1

FULL MOON SHOTS

et me tell you about Molasses." That's how Painter John would generally begin a story—in this case about a giant horseshoe crab. Another might be about Jack and the Beanstalk, or Grandpop Gilligan's pirate sword. The story would also begin with a child on his knee as these were family-friendly tales but could be just as readily enjoyed by adults. Painter John was a master storyteller.

Whatever child happened to be on his knee at the time of the story would listen intently as Painter John spun the tale of the giant horseshoe crab he called Molasses that would leave behind enormous tracks in the sand on the beach. The tracks usually came from the direction of "The Point", the stretch of undisturbed beach covered with clumps of marsh grass beyond where Cove Road came to an abrupt end at the northern boundary of Gandy's Beach.

Molasses was rarely seen, but when it did make an appearance, it was only during the full moon. The kids were told to leave peanuts out for it. Painter never did specify exactly how large this crab was, only that it was giant which was just enough to let a child's vivid imagination take over. It was also not known if the animal was aggressive or benign, only that it was there.

Now, the horseshoe crab is not really a crab at all but closely related to arachnids: spiders. They have their own classification because of their arm-like pincers used for feeding known as chelicerae. They are also one of the oldest animals on the planet, virtually unchanged in over 400 hundred million years. You would think that in that amount of time, they would have learned how to use their spike-like tails to flip themselves over should they become upended, but it hasn't happened, even though that's supposedly one of its primary uses. My children have come to the rescue of many an overturned horseshoe crab that would have become seagull breakfast otherwise. That tail, of which many people have an unfounded fear, is used much more advantageously as a rudder.

This ancient, simple creature is just full of surprises. One unique feature is its blood: it's blue. Blue because it contains copper, unlike human blood which contains iron. Johns Hopkins University physician Freder-

ick Bang discovered that he could use this remarkable blue blood to test if vaccines or injectable drugs were safe to use before dispensing them for human patients. Horseshoe crabs, which were once slaughtered by the thousands for use as fertilizer now happily donate their blood which happens to be worth approximately $15,000 per .750 ml.

It's not surprising to broach the subject of horseshoe crabs at Gandy's Beach, because that is where you will find tons of them every spring. They descend on the Delaware Bay to use it as their boudoir in an annual mating ritual, the result of which is the deposit of millions of aqu-hued eggs, gorged on by various migratory shore birds. The lady crabs are dominant here, on average 25 to 30 percent larger than the males. So, that could mean that Molasses is a giant female horseshoe crab.

We'll just have to wait until the next full moon to find out.

THE FULL MOON FIGURES prominently in a number of Painter John's stories. This one concerns an adventure in which John had purchased a boat in Westville, NJ. It was a wooden Zobel Sea Skiff which he named the *Minnow* and was planning to run it with his friend Charles Fisher to a marina near his house at Gandy's Beach. For the voyage, John's mother made four turkey sandwiches and sealed them up tightly in plastic baggies. They also had a case of beer: Piels, in rust-proof, corrosion-proof, aluminum cans. They eased the *Minnow* out into the Delaware River and headed south, looking forward to a leisurely cruise in a new boat.

Before long, Charles told John that there was water below in the cabin, but John didn't believe him. Eventually he went down to check for himself and sure enough they were taking on water. The bilge pump was quickly overcome, so they started to bail with a five-gallon bucket, but it was a losing battle. John got out an emergency kit and started reading the directions.

The first procedure was to put on life preservers. The next was to take down the American flag and run up an International Distress flag. It blew off. The anchor was dropped, but as they were in the shipping channel, it never hit bottom and they started to drift. Next, John tried blowing an emergency whistle but it was not loud enough to attract anyone's attention so he threw it overboard. He then found a signaling mirror but couldn't get the protective tape off, so that went overboard as well. Orange dye was the next solution, but it only congealed into a large circle and drifted away from the boat. Now the flares came out. The first one wouldn't ignite. Overboard it went. By that time, only the bow of the boat was above water with the two desperate mariners clinging to it.

The only rescue equipment left was one flare. A tugboat appeared in the shipping lane towing a barge. John said to Charles, "This looks like the last chance to me, but I don't know if he can get near us." He added, "We're goin' down, I might as well light it." This time the flare worked, sending an orange cloud around the sinking vessel causing zero visibility. But when the cloud dissipated, it appeared the tugboat had slowed down. Shortly, another boat approached them, apparently alerted by the tugboat. Both men would now have to jump off the nearly submerged *Minnow* to reach the rescue vessel. But Charles refused to leave because Mr. Jenkins had told him if he ever got in trouble not to leave the boat. John pushed him off. They swam to the rescue boat which took them to Cape May, where John's sister came and picked up the two shipwreck survivors.

And to this day, every full moon, the *Minnow* rises from the depths, still carrying the case of Piels in the corrosion-proof cans and the four turkey sandwiches wrapped in plastic.

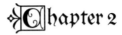

Chapter 2

HOME SWEET WEDGE

here is a piece of real estate once considered a no-man's-land, right in the middle of the original Mid-Atlantic colonies. The area in question is a triangular (or wedge-shaped), 1.068 square mile property that intersects the borders of Pennsylvania, Delaware, and Maryland. For years, it was simply known as "The Wedge."

Part of a grant encompassing the Chesapeake Bay and much of its environs, it was originally awarded to Lord Baltimore, Sir George Calvert in 1632 by Charles I. Unfortunately, Sir George died just weeks before the grant was sealed. The approved charter and title of Lord Baltimore (the 2nd) now fell to his son Caecilius (Cecil) Calvert. Two years later, his younger brother Leonard led some 200 settlers across the Atlantic to found the Maryland colony, a Catholic refuge named for the King's wife, Queen Marietta.

Swedes arrived in 1638 and quietly become squatters on the Calvert claim. The Dutch then took over the Swedish incursion in 1655. Lord Baltimore complained bitterly that they should be removed from his property, but the English crown refused to interfere, fearing the strain it would put on foreign relations.

In 1664, the English took over all Dutch possessions on the Eastern seaboard. Charles II granted to his brother James, the Duke of York, proprietary rights to a massive chunk of land that extended from the St. Croix River at the Canadian border to the Eastern Shore of the Delaware River. The Duke then helped himself to the former Dutch-controlled New Amstel on the Western Shore, which was still technically Lord Baltimore's territory. His explained that he was simply holding it for safekeeping and final control would be advantageous to all concerned. New Amstel became New Castle.

When the Province of Pennsylvania was created for William Penn in 1681, there appeared to be yet more overlapping of the Maryland charter. Penn even sent letters to Maryland landowners in Cecil and Baltimore counties that their taxes should be paid to him and not to Lord Baltimore.

Penn managed to talk the Duke out of New Castle, whose northern boundary was now defined by a twelve-mile arc, allowing Penn access to the Atlantic Ocean via the Delaware River. He also acquired the rest of the current State of Delaware as well. This would lead to territorial disputes between the Penn and Calvert proprietors that would last into the twentieth century.

Nevertheless, in the 1750s the Penns and Calverts did manage to reach an agreement that would try to establish where the boundaries of Pennsylvania, Delaware, and Maryland should be. A bipartisan commission hired surveyors to mark a Transpeninsular Line which determined the southern border of Delaware.

But all this served to do was make things more confusing and vague. Expert help was needed, which is part of the reason that the English team of astronomer Charles Mason & surveyor Jeremiah Dixon was hired to sort things out. They began their task in 1763. Their mission involved determining a Tangent Line, a North Line, the Twelve Mile

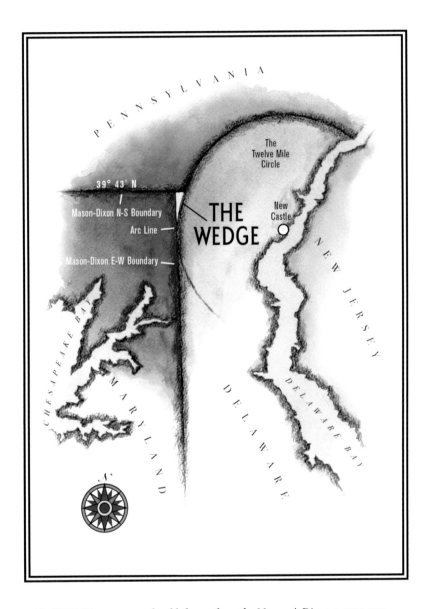

The WEDGE, a no-mans-land left over from the Mason & Dixon survey completed in 1767. It became a hot bed of illicit activity until it was finally awarded to the state of Delaware in 1921.

Circle (the only circular state boundary in the country, centered on the courthouse in New Castle), and longitudinal and latitudinal reckonings.

After four years of exhaustive mapping and surveying, Mason & Dixon returned to England, satisfied with a job well done. They left behind numerous stone markers, quarried from native English limestone, and carried to the colonies to authenticate their work. And everyone in Pennsylvania, Delaware, and Maryland seemed satisfied as well.

It was not until some years later that a tiny, oddly-shaped 800-acre parcel of land could not be accounted for. Delaware assumed ownership, Pennsylvania disputed their claim, but the laws of both states were ignored for the most part. Maryland, possessor of the original charter, was left out of the equation.

In the decades that followed, The Wedge, which also became known as the Flatiron, or Three Corners, acquired a reputation as a refuge for thieves and petty criminals. Gambling, bootlegging, and illegal boxing matches took place, at least one duel was fought, and residents refused to abide by any state regulations. Two generations of Smiths refused to pay taxes to the State of Pennsylvania. Others claimed to have paid taxes to Delaware when the Pennsylvania collectors came calling, and reversed the claim when the Delaware assessors appeared.

Because both states had better things to do, they mostly ignored possession of this insignificant piece of ground. But every once in a while, a new survey would take place, such as the one performed in 1849 by the US Army Corps of Topographical Engineers, that nudged Pennsylvania into claiming the land, and again in 1892 when the Office of the US Coast and Geodetic Survey swung the dispute back in Delaware's favor.

It was not until 1921 that The Wedge was officially, and once and for all, made part of the State of Delaware. The state which for a while, used the tourism tagline "Small Wonder", was no doubt pleased to acquire more land; much of its eastern boundary lies under the Delaware River.

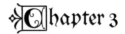

Chapter 3

UNCLE BILL'S

 couple of properties down from Painter John's place was a charming little house on pilings that we all knew as Uncle Bill's. That's because my friend Tubby's Uncle Bill had once owned it. He and his wife were a lovely couple. When I was first introduced to them, Bill made the intimate comment that he had known Tubby since he was "no bigger than a turd in a shoebox."

Uncle Bill had quirky tastes in food. He believed that you could add just about any leftover to spaghetti sauce: lunchmeat, chicken wings, spare ribs, pickles, green beans, sauerkraut, and it would instantly be brought to a whole new level of haute cuisine.

The foraging gene was strong in Uncle Bill. He was known to walk along the beach, and finding a stranded clam, would pop it open, and eat it right on the spot. On one memorable occasion, Painter John had been out fishing when he snagged a conch, which was not what he was going after. But he put it in his bait bucket full of squid, and there it sat in the sun for the remainder of his outing. When he came ashore and was showing off his catch, Bill happened to spot the conch in the bait

"It was a bold man who first ate an oyster."
A quote from seventeenth-century satirist Jonathan Swift.

bucket and said, "I'll take that!" He scooped up the conch and after considerable effort, pulled the meaty part out and ate it right then and there.

Seafood scavenging seems to have come naturally to the old-time residents of Gandy's, perhaps recalling hard times during the Great Depression. Loretta, a neighbor of Uncle Bill's, had a fondness for wild mussels. They could be found growing along the beach attached to clumps of marsh grass, concrete bulkheads, pilings, even on the backs of horseshoe crabs.

One time, a telephone lineman arrived to do some repair work on a pole in front of Loretta's house. She decided to take advantage of the situation and talked the lineman into being her spotter while he was up on the pole, locating horseshoe crabs bearing mussels. She positioned herself on the beach, grabbed the creatures, and pulled off the mussels as the lineman pointed them out to her.

WHEN UNCLE BILL PASSED AWAY (from natural causes) his house was acquired by a young man named Russell. His girlfriend lived with him too. Her name was Tina. We all agreed she was an attractive young lady.

The two pretty much kept to themselves except for an occasional encounter on the beach when Tina was taking her dog for a swim. Russell was in the medical profession and worked odd hours so they didn't share the same social schedule as most other inhabitants of the beach.

Tina's dog was a large female Golden Labrador Retriever that spent a great deal of time on their front screened-in porch. I used to take my dog for a walk every morning and when I passed by Russell's, the two of them exchanged words. It wasn't that they hated each other, in fact they had been nose-to-nose a number of times and the meetings were cordial enough. But sometimes all it takes is attempted encroachment of territory to extract long-forgotten threats and oaths from the dawn of canine time.

At one point, Tina's dog became pregnant and could find no better place to give birth than under Painter John's house. Tina was beside herself. It was only a twelve-inch high crawl space and trying to get her expecting dog to come out proved far more difficult than one might expect. But after a full bag of dog treats and a pound of lunchmeat, the pregnant pooch relinquished her birthing nest for a more suitable spot in Russell's house. It was a typical day at the beach.

▸ ▸ ▸

PAINTER JOHN'S HOUSE had a small, very small, wooden porch attached to the front. It was not even one step up and perched right on the sand.

It wasn't always like that. The house was actually built on pilings, like many other homes at Gandy's. But because of storm damage, Cove Road was continually built up. Then the next storm would wash road

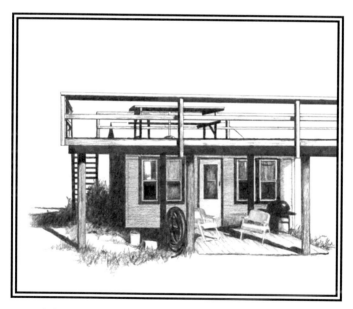

Painter John's house, which was actually the reclaimed second floor of another home located in South Jersey and moved to Gandy's Beach.

gravel under Painter's house. The process kept repeating until his house eventually wound up below street level. He actually had steps when the house was first put in place. Many a night was spent there enjoying a quiet evening, listening to the sound of the water sloshing just across the road, telling stories, sharing hot gossip, discussing the events of the day, the days gone by, and the days yet to come. But not quite as many daylight hours were spent on the little porch, because there were other pressing matters to attend to: yard sales, finding bait, setting the crab traps, fishing, taking trash to the dump, nursing a hangover, or sometimes the all-important task of doing nothing.

One bright beach morning; a little too bright considering the previous evening, I happened to be chatting with Painter John on his tiny front porch. John was facing northwest, I was facing southeast. I noticed movement over his shoulder a little way down Cove Road, which was the main road at Gandy's Beach. In fact it was the only road.

The movement that I noticed came from Russell's house. Something flew out of the front door; it seemed to be an article of clothing. Soon, another article followed the first one, then another, and another; each successive piece seemed to increase in size and weight. A couple of pillows were jettisoned, floating through the air as if in slow motion. Then a pair of shoes, then a piece of luggage, some swimming fins, books, a radio alarm clock, and a small nightstand.

Painter John was chuckling about how his young son "Clammer John" had shown his appreciation for a recent visit from his aunt by putting a couple of shedder crabs under her pillow one evening. Half listening, I craned my neck for a better angle to observe the goings-on at Russell's. I interrupted John's story to point out the commotion, and just as he turned around to get a better look came the grand finale: a twin bed mattress tumbled out of the front door, over the railing of his front porch, and landed with a whump! on the road, kicking up a great cloud of dust.

It seems that objects flung from houses at Gandy's Beach is not that rare an occurence. Another incident involved a gentleman named Walt, who had purchased a new refrigerator that was delivered to his house which was also on Cove Road. All was not right, however, as the automatic ice maker on the fridge was not working. After several futile phone calls trying to reach the service department to complain about the problem, he was finally able to connect with a real person, and a promise was made that a technician would soon arrive to see to the situation.

The next day, a repairman showed up, muttered something under his breath, took out a few tools, and made some minor adjustments. He soon left, satisfied that the problem was taken care of and hightailed it out of town to take advantage of a long Labor Day weekend.

But it seems the refrigerator gnomes had other ideas and, shortly after the repairman left, the problem returned. Walt called for repairs again, but since it was now a holiday weekend, he was informed that no repair service would be available for four more days. The thought of having to spend Labor Day weekend without an ice maker was unthinkable.

Walt's temper was legendary, and his lack of patience was the subject of articles in psychiatric journals. On hearing the news that no repairs would be forthcoming, he began seething. It came to an explosive climax that evening as he was seen wrestling the flawed appliance out of his front door, duck walking it across his deck while grunting like an NFL lineman, and giving it a mighty heave down his steps, thumping each one on its downward journey before coming to rest beside Cove Road.

As for Russell and Tina, I'm not sure what happened between them but after the house clearing row, we never saw Tina again. Russell eventually sold the house and moved on.

The next owner was a woman named Monica who let it be known that she was an actress. She was cautiously polite but had a coarse exterior. My children told me they were afraid of her.

Nearly every house on the beach had an open door policy. You could strike up a friendly chat with someone you were not familiar with, and the next thing you knew, you were in their house sharing beers as if you had been lifelong friends.

But there was none of that with Monica. She never invited anyone into her house, although we did see that she occasionally had visitors who we found out through the grapevine were students.

Once I was walking my dog (as you can tell, I'm a fierce dog walker) and, as we passed by Monica's house, formerly Russell's, formerly Uncle Bill's, I stopped to chat with her for a moment. My dog found some interesting smell on the crushed oyster shells that made up the bulk of Monica's yard. She noticed this, and in mid-sentence stopped and said, "Your dog is on my property" as if she had just finished vacuuming the shells. Maybe the territorial nature of Tina's dog had manifested itself in Monica. I wouldn't have been surprised if her property was mined.

Another oddity occurred one evening when we were strolling along Cove Road heading to Tommy T's house for a visit when we spotted Monica hiding in the shadows underneath a neighbor's deck. "Monica, what are you doing?" we asked. We took her by such complete surprise that she had no choice but to answer truthfully, "I'm spying!" Apparently, she was trying to dig up something illegal on one of the residents of "the Blue House," which I'll bring up again shortly.

Eventually the restorative aura of the beach seemed to have a calming effect on Monica and she became friendlier. You never know what private demons people are battling, but it's amazing what a little R & R next to the soothing waters of the Delaware Bay can do.

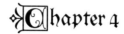

Chapter 4

THE WRITTEN WEDGE

ong, long ago, in a place we were all taught was the Cradle of Civilization, people discovered a most important guideline for engaging in social and business activities: get it in writing. It was just as true then as it is now.

One of the earliest methods of writing was known as cuneiform, from the Latin *cuneus* which means, what else, 'wedge'. It was introduced by Sumerian scribes in the ancient city of Uruk, in today's Iraq around 3200 BCE. Using a wedge-shaped stylus fashioned from a reed, the end was pressed into a clay tablet and manipulated so that different arrangements of the strokes could be combined to form "letters", and further still to create words. The process began as the literal interpretation of animals and objects but progressed to symbolic representations. The strokes could be vertical or horizontal, small, large, or combined in as many as a thousand different arrangements and variations.

Interestingly, most tablets could fit in your hand like a cellphone, and were only intended for short-term use, like a drug dealer's burner. This style of communicating was not a language in itself, but could be adapted to write several languages. It was so versatile that it could no doubt be used even today to write English, Spanish, Russian, French…you get the idea.

As many as two million of these clay tablets have survived which gives us remarkable insight into daily life in the Middle East of thousands of years ago. Recent discoveries have also revealed that certain cuneiform tablets contain complex equations used to calculate astronomical events, and can even predict the motion of Jupiter. Most of them, however, record basic accounting, tallies of grain harvests, births, deaths, and daily minutia. More important records were later chiseled into stone using the same basic techniques.

Sometime after the first century A.D., alphabetic writing came into being, greatly increasing efficiency in the art of visual communication, and cuneiform was gradually forgotten. Nearly 2,000 years later, nineteenth-century archeologists began unearthing the ancient clay tablets and set to the task of deciphering them. It was tedious work, but eventually the old documents gave up their secrets, although some of the most ancient remain unreadable.

The most pronounced tablets told monumental tales of kings and conquests, but the majority were much more commonplace. One in particular seems to prove that human nature has changed very little over the millennia. It is considered the oldest known written complaint, and it's pretty juicy. The missive describes a transaction between a customer known as Nanni, who protested that the copper merchant Ea-Nasir had provided an inferior product; even insulting Nanni's servants:

"What do you take me for, that you treat somebody like me with such contempt? I have sent as messengers, gentlemen like ourselves to collect the bag with my money (deposited with you) but you have treated me with contempt by sending them back to me empty-handed several times, and that through enemy territory. Is there anyone among the merchants who trade with Telmun who has treated me in this way?"

He goes into greater deal about his dissatisfaction and concludes:

> "How have you treated me for that copper? You withheld my
> money bag from me in enemy territory; it is now up to you to re-
> store (my money) to me in full. Take cognizance that (from now
> on) I will not accept here any copper from you that is not of fine
> quality. I shall (from now on) select and take the ingots individ-
> ually in my own yard, and I shall exercise against you my right of
> rejection because you have treated me with contempt."

But as it turns out, that was not the only earliest-known complaint.
Mr. (or however you address him) Ea-Nasir left a trail of disgruntled
customers. Besides peddling inferior copper, he also had shady deal-
ings in kitchenware, real estate, used clothing, and more, prompting
hundreds of angry tablets, which, amazingly, he carefully preserved in a
dedicated room in his own house like trophies. Shysterism, apparently,
is timeless.

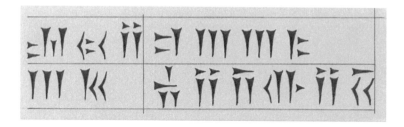

An example of cuneiform writing which, illustrated here, cleverly spells
out the name of this book.

❖ⓒhapter 5

THE TALL SHIP

he Delaware Bay and River were graced by a "Parade of Sail" in June of 1992, as more than a dozen tall ships from around the world arrived to take part in the Philadelphia Columbus 500 celebration. The stately vessels were greeted by cannon salutes, fireboat sprays, and foghorns as they neared Penn's Landing. After a long weekend during which the ships were open to the public who gleefully swarmed over them like so many ants, the ships set sail again for New York City and Boston to continue the festivities. The return voyage took them back down The Delaware once more into the Bay and out through the twin capes to the Atlantic Ocean.

One late afternoon I happened to be at Gandy's Beach, scanning the horizon over the Delaware Bay, which is impossible *not* to do when a large body of water is the most obvious thing in view. I spotted far to the northwest what appeared to be the tops of masts just emerging over the horizon. Gradually I could make out yardarms as well. After spending a few years viewing this body of water at all times of the day and in all kinds of weather conditions, you get to know what different types of ships look like as they gradually rise above the distant waterline. The most dramatic views to me were always on a sunny summer morning when the first visible part of a vessel that could be made out was the bridge lit up by the golden glow of the rising sun. Then the rest of the ship would gradually become more visible, getting closer and closer as it slowly made its way up the shipping channel.

Other than small recreational sailboats on the Bay, you don't see large vessels with more than one mast very often, so when I spotted the unmistakable silhouettes, I immediately surmised that it must be one of the tall ships on its return passage to the Atlantic.

I quickly walked over to Painter John's house to tell him about the approaching tall ship, and he shuffled out onto the sandy road squinting in the direction I had pointed out. He said "Oh yeah. Why don't we take the boat out and go see it?"

And just like that, a plan came together, as they often did at the beach; Painter John had a boat, I had a camera. We could cruise out on the Bay and get some dramatic close-ups of a tall ship. He said, "Let's go!" My wife, Painter John, and myself all jumped into his Ford Crown Victoria LTD with fake wood sides and a way-back seat and off we went. He turned on the radio from which, seemingly on cue, "Legs", by ZZ Top started playing—the perfect traveling music for easily amused people on a mission. He pumped up the volume and we started dancing in our seats.

Painter John moored his boat *Stormy* at the Money Island marina, which was actually less than a mile away, but on the other side of Beach Creek, requiring a drive of about three miles to get to it. It only took a few minutes, however; they are not busy roads. We pulled up to the marina, jumped out of the station wagon, and started to make the boat ready. Soon we were heading out of Nantuxent Creek, then across Nantuxent Cove and out onto the bay. John gunned it full throttle and *Stormy* trimmed out perfectly as the tall ship was now well within view,

A tall ship, making its way south on the Delaware Bay.

although nearly a mile away. I readied my camera, an old Nikon analog, and got ready to start shooting. I can't recall which ship it was, it would have been hard to tell anyway, unless we swung around the stern to the see her nameplate.

Unfortunately, the ship was not under sail, which would have provided exceptionally picturesque photos. As authentic as the tall ships are, nearly all are equipped with auxiliary motors which are requisite for sailing ships these days. And since it was in the shipping lane, there was undoubtedly a regulation against using sails. It would have also been under the command of an authorized Delaware River pilot.

As our Captain, Painter John brought us up as close to the ship as was safely possible and one of the crew perched high up on a mast on the tall ship waved to us. We were thrilled to be acknowledged and, of course, waved back. It was exciting and exhilarating. I went below and stood on the bunks while poking up through the forward hatch, trying to steady myself for what I hoped would be some award-winning photos. I waited patiently until I was sure I would get the perfect shot and pressed the shutter. I hit the advance lever for the next shot and…nothing happened. The film was not advancing. I tried again. Still nothing. A magic moment lost to posterity because of technical failure.

I was sorely disappointed that I couldn't get any photos, especially since you rarely get to see these types of ships on the bay, but we enjoyed our boat ride, nonetheless. We made our way back to Gandy's, enjoyed a spectacular sunset, and recounted our little adventure.

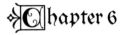

Chapter 6

SAND WEDGE

ur next wedge is associated with the game of golf, which Mark Twain knowingly proclaimed is "a good walk spoiled." Almost from its inception, the game has infuriated players because of the golf ball's maddening habit of refusing to go where you want it to. Hitting it straight is undoubtedly one of the most troublesome parts of the game. Making it go into the hole is another. Staying on the fairway is yet another, and on, and on.

As if those aspects of the game were not cruel enough, another layer of frustration is added—the hazard. There are water hazards which, as the name represents, consist of either a lake, or a stream, or on a few exotic courses, the ocean. There are also sand hazards, or sand traps, referred to as bunkers: pits of sand diabolically positioned to attract any shot that strays off course like a magnet. Of these, there are fairway bunkers, greenway bunkers, and waste bunkers.

And thanks to the warped and sadistic tendencies of golf course architects, there may be more than one hazard per hole. As a former caddie, I have seen many a duffer land in a sand trap and, after numerous attempts, finally manage to blast their way out, only to find their ball has bounced off the green and into another bunker on the opposite side. This is when expensive golf clubs can become missiles hurled in anger.

But there is salvation for those who find themselves in one of these sinister pits of despair. The sand wedge is one member of a family of golf clubs specifically designed to dig the ball out of soft sand, if you know how to wield it correctly.

The sand wedge was invented by famed pro golfer Gene Sarazen in 1931. Sarazen based his new club on the ancient pitching iron, the "niblick." By adding extra lead to the sole of the club head and adjusting the angle, the new wedge was prevented from getting too far under the ball or sending it bouncing along the top of the sand. It must have worked pretty well because he won both the British and US Open tournaments in 1932. He kept his secret weapon hidden from the officials, fearing that they might rule it illegal. It was, however, sanctioned by the both the R&A and the USGA eventually, and then copied by club manufacturers.

The wedge is not only good for digging the ball out of a sand trap, but when the ball lands after a lofty trajectory, it is far less likely to bounce or roll any great distance. If you've ever watched a pro golf tournament, this is a shot that draws satisfying murmurs of approval from the fans as the balls drops dead just a few feet from the hole.

Aside from the niblick, there were other colorful Scottish terms used to describe the clubs that have unfortunately gone extinct: Brassie, Spoon, Mashie, Spade mashie, Mashie-niblick, Baffy, Cleek, Lofter, and Jigger. Driver and Putter remain but the others are now identified simply by boring numbers.

These hand-crafted wooden clubs were used to smack wooden balls, which gave way to leather orbs stuffed with compressed bird feathers. In 1848 the gutta percha ball was introduced. Known as a "gutty", it was made from dried gum resin produced by the Malaysian sapodilla tree. The modern golf ball arrived in the early twentieth-century, and is still

being improved upon. Although no one has of yet installed a homing signal to locate the ones that have somehow become lost.

Although early forms of attempting to skillfully hit a ball with a club have indeterminate origins, the game of golf or "gouf" has been associated with the Scots since the early fourteenth-century, eventually becoming an accepted pastime. However, archers took the game so seriously that they could more often be found on the links rather than honing their skills with the bow. Since their craft was so vital to the defense of Scotland, the game was made a criminal offense, punishable by hanging. James II banned the sport in 1457.

But the ban was largely ignored and gradually evolved into the modern version. In 1502, it was officially sanctioned when the first recorded game was played between James IV and the Earl of Bothwell. Golf quickly gained popularity and spread throughout Europe as Charles I introduced the joys of the links to the English; Mary Queen of Scots brought it to France when she traveled there for studies.

The first eighteen-hole course was constructed at the town of St. Andrews, Scotland in 1764. Long considered the ancestral home of the game, it probably did not originate there, but is officially known as the Royal and Ancient Golf Club of St. Andrews. It is the standard for all eighteen-hole courses.

The hazards themselves grew out of the naturally bleak, desolate conditions that are common to Scotland, particularly around St. Andrews. Sheep found depressions in the terrain and burrowed into the turf to keep them out of the cold, harsh wind. Eventually, the depressions became larger and deeper. The "bunkers" became such an accepted feature of the landscape that they were included in the early courses and eventually filled with sand. They became more imaginatively insidious as the game evolved.

According to "The Golf Professor", the best way to punch out of a bunker is to "try squaring your feet and shoulders to the target line, then take a normal swing, concentrating on maintaining a smooth tempo from start to finish." Or, forget golf, and take up a less stressful sport, like bullfighting.

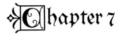

No Turnaround

Gandy's Beach was never a tourist attraction like Ocean City, Wildwood, Sea Isle City, or other Jersey seashore destinations. There was nothing there but houses strung out along one gravel road that ran parallel to the Delaware Bay. No restaurants, bars, clubs, mini-golf courses, or even a boardwalk. The water and a primal fascination with it were the main attraction. There was not much traffic on Cove Road. A lone bicyclist, someone strolling, or the occasional surplus golf cart driven by either a giggling teenager with a bunch of friends, or a shirtless guy with a beer. It was such a tiny closely-knit community that when someone did drive by, the nosier residents, ourselves included, would peer out their windows to see who was intruding.

Golf carts are not street legal. However, there was one Gandy's resident who did manage to push the limit. The gentleman, whose name was Victor, decided to drive his golf cart one Saturday morning from Gandy's to Fortescue, another bayshore community. It was a distance of about six miles, using Fortescue Road, a winding rural road with no shoulders and heavily trafficked by fishermen in a hurry to make their way out onto the water before all the fish were caught.

Victor, regardless of owning a house on Cove Road, seemed to live around the corner from everyone else. He especially did not endear himself to women and rarely missed an opportunity to express his sexist views, particularly to his wife and especially when he had an audience. He was once asked his nationality by an astute visitor to his home. He replied that he was Polish and Russian, to which the visitor remarked, "So you like to drink, but you don't know why."

When Victor arrived at Fortescue after nearly being run off the road by a number of annoyed drivers, he pulled into the parking lot of Higbee's Luncheonette, across the street from Higbee's Marina.

He sat at the counter, ordered breakfast, and immediately began harassing the waitress, making remarks about how she was in the right profession, waiting on men, and how women belonged in the kitchen, and the usual sexist diatribe. The waitress took it in stride, however, as she was used to dealing with crusty fishermen. His trash-talking was not lost on Betty Higbee however, the owner of the establishment, who had been aware of his ranting the whole time. When Victor was finished with his food, she approached him and asked if he enjoyed it. Victor replied that it was fine, and Betty said, "Good, because that's the last meal you'll ever get in this place!"

And now for the just deserts. After Victor left Fortescue in his golf cart, he was pulled over by an NJ State Trooper. The trooper made him push the golf cart off the road, gave him a serious reprimand, and a hefty traffic citation, after which Victor had to walk back to Gandy's. He couldn't find anyone with a flatbed truck, so he had to rent one and talk some friends into loading the golf cart for transport back to his house. That cost him several cases of beer. (For a while after the incident, it was rumored that the police had been tipped off concerning Victor's error in judgement but it was quickly dismissed when no one could imagine who might do a thing like that.)

ON WEEKENDS DURING the height of the summer, there could be a small but steady stream of sightseers out for a drive. For most of them, it was disappointing, especially when it was discovered that Cove Road was a dead-end. They would have to perform an awkward turn-around in a limited amount of space in front of Tommy T's house and head back the same way they came in.

There was a house a few properties to the north of ours that everyone called the Bird House. It had once been a real estate office located elsewhere in South Jersey, then moved to Gandy's and placed on pilings. It became known as the Bird House because although it was a simple, square structure, it had a lot of windows, a cupola on top, and was painted a garish purple. This seemed odd because the owner, whose name was Jim, was a professional house painter. Maybe the paint was left over from one of his jobs.

Most Gandy's residents simply put up with the increased traffic, it was a public road after all. But not Birdhouse Jim. He was annoyed and decided to do something about it. One day, a sign appeared on the edge of his property. It was a typical official-looking bright-red octagonal stop sign, which did indeed read STOP, but also: NO TURN AROUND.

It produced the desired effect. Sightseers would heed the sign and turn their cars around to go back the way they came. But this created a new problem. The cars were turning around in front of Jim's neighbor's house, creating a disturbance during an otherwise peaceful and quiet day. We knew the neighbors. Their house was painted blue, which we took to calling the Blue House. (Everything gets reduced to its basic elements at the beach.) They were a fun-loving group from Northeast Philly who enjoyed late-night parties. They were quiet during the day, however, recuperating from the previous night's festivities. But frequent k-turns in front of their house while they were in recovery mode proved to be a problem that could not be ignored. They complained but the sign stayed in place. We assumed there would be repercussions.

The turnarounds continued for the next week or so, until one Saturday night the Blue House folks were a little more raucous than usual, their revelry spilling out of their house and onto the road. We had our own houseful and were pre-occupied with our own merriment for most of the evening until everyone was spent and we eventually all went to bed. I was still aware of the neighbors outside but I drifted off as their voices slowly faded away.

The next morning I walked out onto the road to take stock of the day. It was typically gorgeous, and the bay smelled like watermelon. The beach in front of our house was clear with no pilings, rocks, or obstructions, just the Delaware Bay for miles. Which is why I looked twice when I noticed something poking out of the water in front of the Birdhouse. I thought it must just be some debris floating by. I went back into our house and made some breakfast. We had a wonderful view of the bay from our dining table; I even saw dolphins swimming by one morning. I could still see the object in the water, which had not drifted at all, and as the tide was going out, there was gradually more and more of it. I could eventually even make out its color: red.

After breakfast, my curiosity peaked and I stepped outside again and walked a short distance up the road to get a better look at the object in the water. It was a red sign for sure and the word STOP was just beginning to become visible. Realizing what had happened, I turned to find Painter John walking towards me grinning from ear to ear. "Must have been some party", he snickered. Apparently, Birdhouse Jim's neighbors had taken custody of his NO TURN AROUND sign and planted it in the bay at high tide. It stayed there for some time until it became completely exposed, providing amusement for many locals and sightseers, and embarrassment for Birdhouse Jim.

I could not tell you what was said during the exchange that took place between Birdhouse Jim and his neighbors after he discovered what had happened to his sign. It was eventually retrieved from the Bay and returned to its rightful owner. But I think Jim must have gotten the message because the NO TURN AROUND sign was never seen again, either on land or sea.

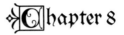

Chapter 8

WEDGES & FEATHERS

ave you ever walked along a stone jetty and noticed holes in the massive rocks? Or that one of the rocks has been split and you can see a series of grooves along the break? Those features are evidence of how stone is purposely fractured.

Stone seems to be the most indestructible material on earth, or the universe, for that matter. But like any super power, it has its weaknessess. The kryptonite for rocks is its tensile strength. Huge blocks of stone can be piled on top of each other like the pyramids, and they'll stay like that seemingly forever. But they can be pulled apart like cotton candy. Well, not quite that easily, but in terms of hard stuff, a simple wedge can force a large boulder into submission.

Here's how it works, basically. It's a hands-on technique that involves drilling holes along a natural seam or grain in the rock. Depending on the size of the stone to be divided, multiple holes may have to be drilled. Metal implements known as "wedges and feathers" are inserted into the holes and pounded in succession until the rock starts to split. The technique may seem simple, but it's really not. Some expertise is required along with familiarity with various types of rock. The feathers are shims with flanges at the top which are inserted into the holes, with the flanges

HOW IT WORKS

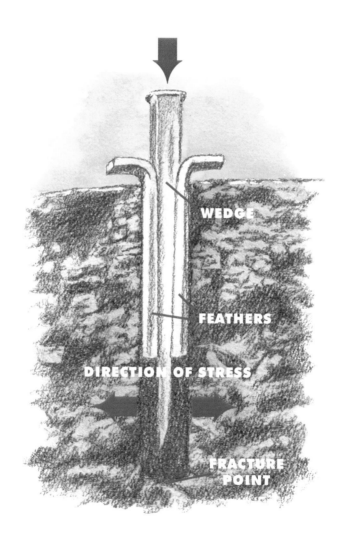

facing the intended direction of the split. The wedge is inserted between the feathers and pounded in. Because the wedge is tapered, it forces the feathers apart, putting stress on the rock. This doesn't happen imme-diately. As the wedges are struck, the sound begins to change as they tighten, then a pause is required as the stone reacts to the pressure. The person, or persons, doing the grunt work steps back and lets nature take its course. A crack will appear, either on its own, or with more coaxing. Now all that remains is moving two large rocks.

Similar methods date to the time of the ancient Egyptian civiliza-tions, who we know were extremely fond of stone. Their tools were a lit-tle more primitive, though. Instead of drilling holes, they were forced to create grooves with chisels and mallets, then insert bronze wedges. Ob-viously, that was much more labor and time-intensive, but they didn't seem to mind, judging from the amount of antiquities they left behind.

Since stone is such a durable construction material, and there's still so much of it around, it has never really gone out of style. But mod-ern large-scale industrial projects demand cheaper and more efficient methods of harvesting. The most practical method is to simply blast the rocks apart, but the results are haphazard. Explosives are used primarily for very hard rocks like granite, basalt, quartz, gneiss, and the like. For more precise extraction, mechanized hammer drills are applied which also use wedges, but on a much larger scale. This is the technique for quarrying those large boulders used for jetties and the like that need to be of roughly equal size. Extremely large machines called Channelizers are employed in extracting expensive stuff like marble. Equipped with reciprocating cutting tools, they can cut out enormous blocks with pre-cision accuracy.

Space-age chemical technology has now entered the equation as well in the form of expanding concrete, also known as demolition grout. It is a highly efficient form of rock breaking without using heavy equipment, and much cheaper. Holes are drilled in the desired area, water is added to the grout mix and then poured into the holes. As the mixture sets, it expands, producing approximately 18,000 psi of force. Inevitably, the rock succumbs. Could this spell the end of wedges and feathers?

*"Give me six hours to chop down
a tree and I will spend the first
four sharpening the blade."*
- A. Lincoln

▰ ▰ ▰

ASIDE FROM SPLITTING STONE, wedges can also be used for the age-old chore of splitting wood for the fire. We've all seen the required segment in old westerns of some burly sodbuster in a plaid shirt and suspenders setting a log on a stump and splitting it in half with one mighty swing from his trusty axe. Well, that's one way of doing it, but according to those in the know, including Bob Vila, the best way to split wood is not with an axe, but with a splitting maul, which is more like an axe with a wedge-shaped head. You may also need an actual wedge or two for those stubborn gnarly limbs. You will also need a chopping block to set your intended log on and, I'm not kidding, an old car tire. Set your log in the middle of the tire and it will keep it in place should you miss; it will also keep pieces from falling all over the place.

However, for those who would rather avoid the unpleasant prospect of physical labor but enjoy noise and drama, try a black powder wedge and blast your logs apart. A hollow wedge is loaded with black powder, driven into a log and then a lit fuse is inserted into the side. Stand back, insert fingers in ears, and wait for the same effect as if participating in an eighteenth-century naval battle. Experts advise us that just a couple hundred grains of powder are all that is necessary. Oh, and don't stand behind the log being exploded. There could be unexpected consequences.

If you seriously need to chop a lot of wood, forget the manual labor and get yourself a hydraulic log splitter, the business end of which is still…a wedge. So remember, for your next patio project, re-creating a Michelangelo masterpiece, or providing fuel for your fire, start with a wedge.

 **Chapter 9**

MOM'S

he words "Mom's Place" were hand-painted, orange, on a weathered board nailed to a couple of pilings that stood next to Fortescue Road, which wound its way to Gandy's Beach. That's where you could get the freshest and most reasonably priced live blue crabs in the area. The only thing better was to catch them yourself. The owners had their own crab boat and by around ten or eleven o'clock on most summer mornings would bring in their catch packed in wooden bushel baskets. They were filled with number ones and number twos. Number ones were the largest-sized crabs and the most popular. They sold out very quickly.

Number twos were occasionally "girls": female crabs that are not as large as the males and that some connoisseurs feel do not have as much meat. There has long been controversy over the harvesting of female crabs, from both a legal and ethical point of view. But in New Jersey and Delaware, there is no law against catching or eating females. Only size matters: 4.5" for hard shells, and 3.5" for soft shells. If you really want to know the difference between male and female blue crabs, just look underneath—very carefully. The males have an "apron" which is compared in shape to the Washington Monument, and the female, in keeping with

the same analogy, has an apron like the Capitol dome. Another determining factor is the color of the claws: bright blue for the males, and red
tips on the females, like nail polish.

Cumberland County, New Jersey is the poorest in the state; its taxes
are half of what the rest of New Jersey's residents pay. Much of that is
due to the collapse of the oyster industry in the 1950s which, although
on the upswing today, has never truly recovered to the state of its former salad days. Some of the region's inhabitants still work the bay by
crabbing part-time, which means you have to have a boat. Everybody
knows boats take money, but rarely make money. A crabber has to own
a decent amount of crab pots to make it worthwhile; maybe 100. But a

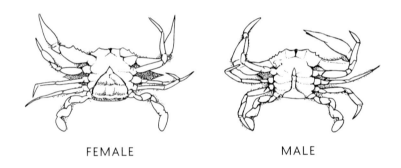

FEMALE   MALE

license is also required for every crab pot, so that could add up. Then
there's the cost of bait for every pot, which, according to the NJDEP
Division of Fish and Wildlife, must be checked and emptied of all crabs
and organisms at least once every 72 hours. It's a lot of work. Most crabbers sell their harvest to retailers, but Mom's eliminated the middle-man
and sold directly to their customers. Location was the key.

Many sport fishermen drove right by Mom's on their way to Fortescue or Gandy's on weekends and were always on the lookout for bait.
Shedder crabs were the classic lure: small crabs that have molted and

not had a chance to grow a new exoskeleton. Fish find them particularly appealing. Mom's would occasionally have them; if not, fishermen would have to resort to paying market prices at nearby Jenkin's Seafood Store, or even higher prices at Fortescue. And, for that reason, many hopeful fishermen would stop at Mom's and ask for shedders. Those who worked at Mom's were quiet and accommodating folks who didn't have a lot to say, but the constant questioning began to wear on their patience. Their solution to the problem was another hand-painted sign that simply said "yes." That meant they had shedder crabs. If the sign was not there, they did not.

Most people cook crabs by simply dumping them into a large pot of boiling water with some crab seasoning like Old Bay, put a lid on it, and wait for about twenty minutes for them to be done. That's the traditional method wherever blue crabs are found. But on the Delaware Bay–the New Jersey side–crab grazing was handled differently. Folks there would clean the crabs before cooking, which means ripping off the back and removing the vitals of the crab. The ladies in particular preferred this method because they didn't like dealing with the yucky innards.

But that created an entirely different problem. Live crabs are extremely bad-tempered and feisty and don't like to have their backs pulled off. Their pincers are very powerful and if they got hold of you, onlookers would think you were dancing the Watusi. That part of the job was usually turned over to the men. We tried various techniques for calming the doomed critters before they were ripped asunder, such as putting them in a bucket of lukewarm fresh water for a few minutes. This seemed to be the best method but trying to wrangle them into the bucket would take some expertise, often resulting in sliced-up fingers and thumbs.

After the crabs were cleaned, the traditional boiling method was applied, except that a lot of garlic and butter was added to the cooking water. Old Bay was often not used at all. Lots of bread was passed around to sop up the juice. They were good, but to me, whole crabs seem to have more flavor.

Eating them is a messy affair, but soul-satisfying. Even if you don't like crabs, and I know very few people in that category, the social aspects alone are therapeutic. Not much is needed for the total experience either; no formal dinnerware or place settings required; only your fingers. Little wooden mallets or nut crackers are sometimes offered, but most serious crab eaters don't even use them.

THE CHESAPEAKE BAY REGION is famed for its seafood restaurants where cooked crabs are spread out on newspapers over sturdy tables and everybody digs in. The New Jersey bayshore had none of that. However, once every summer, the Bonanza II, a fishing and party boat from Fortescue, was chartered to take a large group of Gandy's residents across the Delaware Bay and up the Leipsic River in Delaware. The river winds its way through the 16,000 acre Bombay Hook National Wildlife

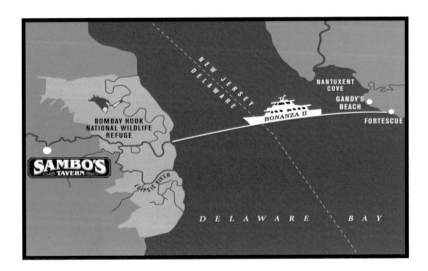

Refuge, a massive wetlands preserve that is home to migratory birds and other types of wildlife.

The boat pulled up to Sambo's Tavern, founded in 1953 by Samuel "Sambo" Burrows, a farm boy turned crabber. Our noisy crowd would file in, thrilled to be away from the kids for an evening, exhilarated by our excursion, and ready for an outing of bad jokes, beer, and a fun-filled eating orgy.

Dining at Sambo's was not an elegant experience, nor should it have been. But the place did have its own ambiance; rows of tables covered with the requisite newspaper and bare wooden floors. Before the meal, we mingled and hovered over the tables like it was a school lunchroom, but when giant trays of steaming crabs began to arrive, it was down to business.

At frequent intervals during the feeding frenzy, some happy eater would invariably call out, "look at this one!", holding up a thumb-size chunk of snow-white crab meat. This would continue for hours, the din of crab claws cracking and people eating and talking until at last the carnage was over and there was nothing left but enormous piles of crustacean debris on the tables and diners with little bits of pink shell clinging to the corners of their mouths.

The return voyage was just as enjoyable as the initial trip, except the night added a dreamy quality to the bay. Twinkling lights guided us home, especially the yard sale Christmas lights that decorated the front porch of our house.

FOR THOSE WHO ENJOY eating crabs, you are in no way limited to buying them at a retail source. Non-commercial licenses for a crab pot are available from the DEP but you really don't even need a license to catch crabs in New Jersey. They just need to be the legal size, and you're limited to one bushel per day. That's a lot of crabs. The easiest method for catching your own, and probably the most fun, is hand lining. All you need is some string and some bait. Fishing line works best, but butcher's twine or household string will do the job. Chicken necks make excellent bait, but almost any kind of meat or fish product that is past its prime will do; crabs are bottom feeders after all. You could use a couple more things as well: a weight to make your line sink to the bottom, and a net or tongs to grab the crab when it comes to the surface.

You don't have to hook the crab like you do with a fish; when you feel a tug, just slowly pull your line up and when the crab is just out of the water, slide your net under it, or grab it with tongs and haul it in. Crabs are tenacious and greedy creatures, so you don't really have to worry too much about them sensing danger and letting go. They're yours.

A FRIEND OF MINE once jokingly speculated that Mom's was probably a chain, that every location had the same homey back-yard look, with the same artfully distressed sign that was designed to exacting specifications by some PR firm in New York. That's how jaded we were.

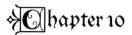

Chapter 10

PIE WEDGE

ie. Mmm…generally served in slices, but occasionally referred to as a wedge because of the shape. Nearly anything that is round can be divided into wedges because it's the most logical way to create equal portions, unless of course the pie is divided in half, in which case you no longer have a wedge.

Columnist George Will wrote a short article in the Washington Post back in 1981 called The Pie-Wedge Principle. In it, he stated that a female acquaintance from Illinois would really get her nose out of joint if a waiter had the audacity to serve her a piece of pie that did not have the point of the wedge facing directly at her.

I believe the article implies that the point directs you to the much bigger picture, and if it is off-kilter, then that's just one of many adjustments you have to deal with before you make it to the crust. However, he also attached moral issues to the analogy: the limiting of government spending, society living off its seed corn, the crumbling of the sacred institution of marriage, and many other societal woes. My advice: eat the crust first.

At some point in the past, 1801 to be exact, a gentleman by the name of William Playfair also did something analogous with a pie. He used it as a symbolic graphic to demonstrate statistics. He didn't use a real pie of course; as a Scot, his mother would have swatted him senseless. Instead, he drew an illustration of a pie and divided the wedges into various sized portions to indicate data; in this case, he was representing the Turkish Empire's landholdings. While he was at it, he also invented the bar chart.

The Scots have had a profound influence on mathematical and technical affairs. As Samuel Johnson so astutely noted: "Much may be made of a Scotsman if he's caught young."

Playfair's proto-pie chart sat ignored for about fifty years before being unearthed by French engineer Charles Joseph Minard, who elaborated on the concept and used it to demonstrate amounts and proportions of butcher's meats supplied to Paris. At about the same time, English nurse and statistician Florence Nightingale used a variation known as a polar area diagram in which all the wedges have the same angle but extend to different perimeters from the center. She was plotting the causes of deaths in the British Army during the Crimean War.

In the modern era, pie charts have become one of the most popular visualization techniques used to demonstrate data. The basics have remained the same but have been elaborated on. In addition to Nightingale's diagrams, other variations have evolved including Spie Charts, Radial Charts, 3D Pie Charts, Doughnut Charts, and the infamous Exploding Pie in The Face Chart.

But experts like to point out that pie charts are evil. The reason is that humans have trouble comparing angles, and that bar charts are much easier on our tender visual capabilities. Information technologist Stephen Few points out that the "pie chart's colorful voice is often heard, but rarely understood. It mumbles when it talks." American mathematician John Wilder Turkey stated that, "There is no data that can be displayed in a pie chart that cannot be displayed better in some other type of chart."

Since pie charts have surpassed the saturation point, they have been heartily welcomed into the world of memes. Personal reflection, social commentary, cat behavior, practically anything can be charted. Here are a couple of my humble entries.

HOW PUBLISHING
PROFITS ARE SHARED

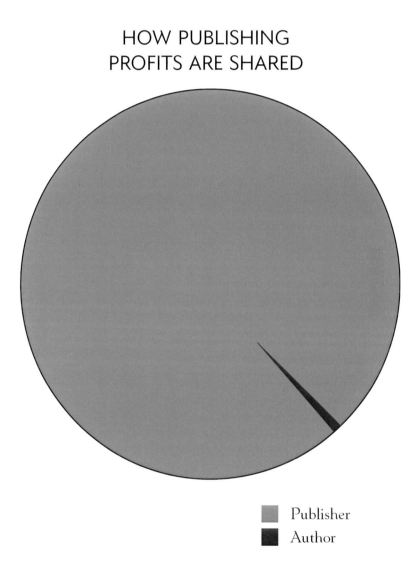

■ Publisher
■ Author

A WRITER'S DAY

Feed cats (morning)	Lunch
Clean litter pan	Nap
Breakfast	Miscellaneous chores
Exercise	Write
Type sudden inspiration into latest manuscript	Feed cats (evening)
Go for a walk	Happy hour
Check emails	Dinner
Browse internet	After dinner

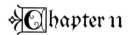

LOCAL COLOR

ll of Painter John's stories featured lots of local color and would vary with each telling, only vaguely following the original storyline; like Jack and The Beanstalk. The family cow was obtained from "old man Estadt", who had a farm on Cedarville Road. (The Estadts turned the front of their old farmhouse into a popular produce stand, handing out lollipops to the children of customers). Other versions didn't mention the cow's origins, it was just the family cow. After Jack's mother instructed him to sell the cow for food, he walked to Barnett's gas station in his "Viet-naaam sandals" (another telling might have Jack wearing Johnny Cornstalker boots), but was instead coerced into trading it for magic beans. When his mother found out about the magic beans, she was so mad she threw them out—in the lot behind Jenkin's Seafood store in Newport where the giant beanstalk started to grow, as Painter John pointed out, "…because it had the seafood smell."

The story would continue in this fashion, and when the part came about Jack's discovery in the giant's house, Painter would loudly bellow, "Fee, fi, fo, fum, I smell the breath of a damn Irishmon!" If the pee wee audience had begun to falter, his outburst would immediately startle

them back to attention. And all the grownups would laugh.

Next came some family history. It was known that Grandpop Gilligan was a pirate; he had sailed with Blackbeard and Captain Kidd. And then Painter John would pull out Grandpop Gilligan's sword (which was an old Knights of Columbus ceremonial piece). It was tarnished and had dark spots where the finish had worn off. John told his young listeners that it was blood from all the battles he had fought sinking ships and capturing gold doubloons during his career as a pirate. The children would stare in fascination at the stains on the sword. The story evolved and was modified during each telling.

ANOTHER TALE (this one for the grownups) involved a visit to the Seabreeze Tavern with his friend Irv. Seabreeze was originally known as Ben Davis' Beach. There was a small public house there utilized by local inhabitants, while other visitors slept in tents and wagons. Then in 1877, the Delaware Steamboat Company built a forty-room resort hotel that they called the Fox Chase, supposedly after sport hunting of the sly creatures. Aside from the guest rooms, there were parlors, a billiard room, and a kitchen featuring "all the delicacies of the season, such as Terrapins, Fish, Oysters &c." The main attraction, however, was "a fine, white sandy beach one mile in extant for bathing, free from dangerous undertows, stingrays, and sharks." The resort also featured a stable, bath houses and bowling alleys, and a merry-go-round.

It became a destination for vacationers escaping the heat and foul summer air in Wilmington and Philadelphia, arriving on the former Civil War supply steamboat the *John A. Warner.* Because of the ship's regular stops throughout the season, the Fox Chase name was cast aside, and the hotel simply became known as the Warner House.

Just before the start of the summer season of 1890 a fire started in the hotel's dining room and quickly spread throughout the building. The

The John A. Warner, *an iron-hulled steamboat, was built in 1857 at the Harlan & Hollingsworth shipyard in Wilmington. It was commandeered during the Civil War to carry supplies and ammunition and to transport wounded Union troops to the federal hospital in Beverly, New Jersey.*

hotel was completely destroyed "and not a stitch or stick of any kind was saved", according to the Bridgeton Evening News.

A little over ten years later, a one-armed trapper and teetotaler named Jessie Smith opened the Seabreeze Hotel. It, too, eventually burned to the ground in the 1940's. But, while it was still in operation, a rival establishment was opened by Harry Griffith in 1929. He called it, appropriately enough, the Seabreeze Tavern. As much as Smith was an abstainer, Griffith was just as equally an advocate, and Smith hated him for it. To make matters even more derisive, Smith had unknowingly sold Griffith the land for his bar through a third party.

In 1945 Griffith's daughter Mae began working at the tavern on the weekends and eventually took over its operation, adding food service which included her much-touted crab cakes.

One evening, Painter John asked Irv to take a ride to the Seabreeze Tavern. But Irv's wife, fearing it had a reputation, would not allow him to go to such a place. So they decided on an innocent boat ride instead. The two men got into Painter's boat, headed south, and when they were out of sight of Gandy's, made a u-turn and headed for Seabreeze. The tavern and Seabreeze itself were accessible by a single road that zig-zagged through the marsh from Fairton, or boaters could tie up at a small marina, as the tavern sat right on the water.

When Painter John and Irv arrived at the Seabreeze Tavern, they secured the boat and entered the place barefoot. A band comprised of old-timers was playing, and John and Irv made themselves right at home. John described drinking and dancing with the women and said he didn't know what Irv was doing, but he was having a good time.

They stayed until the place closed, but the party spilled outside and whiskey was passed around in paper cups. John and Irv naturally joined in. By the time they finally went back to the boat, they were as drunk as…

drunken sailors. By now the tide had gone out, and the boat was hanging from the bowline nearly at a ninety-degree angle. In the process of trying to release the line, John fell off the dock and into the black mud of the marina. After flailing around in the muck and becoming completely coated in black ooze, he managed to climb out of the mud and cut the line which sent the boat flopping into the water with a loud splat.

It was now 5 am. After a lengthy series of awkward maneuvers, John managed to steer out of the marina. Making their way back home, Irv said, "You better watch out for the crab pots!" Painter replied, "It don't make any difference... neither one of us can see 'em anyway!" Miraculously, they avoided becoming entangled in crab pot lines. Arriving at Gandy's Beach Marina tired, muddy, and still drunk, they got themselves and the boat cleaned up just as the sun was coming up over the yardarm.

The Seabreeze Tavern eventually followed the demise-ridden pattern of its neighbors, only instead of fire, it was destroyed by Hurricane Gloria in 1985.

OUR PLACE AT GANDY'S BEACH was on one side of Painter John's house, and on the other side lived Uncle Jake and Aunt Edie. I remember the first time I was introduced to Jake. He was extremely soft-spoken; you had to listen carefully when he was speaking. One would think he would have gotten tired of people asking him to repeat himself, but he was quite patient. Perhaps that quality was what gave him a reputation as a superb fisherman.

He pulled out an ancient leather wallet and asked if I wanted to see a picture of him as a young boy. I couldn't imagine why he would want to show me a childhood photo of himself, but I didn't want to appear rude and said "Yeah, sure." He slid out of the wallet a photo of a boy, maybe ten or twelve years old with an outlandishly giant penis. We all cracked up over the absurdity of the picture. Jake had obviously played this joke on unsuspecting individuals many times before, and, apparently, it not never got old. If he carried that picture around today he would be arrested.

Painter John said Jake was such a good fisherman that he would catch ten fish to anyone else's one. Whenever he had a guest on his boat, he would allow the guest to be the first one to catch a fish. But when the guest did actually hook a fish and proudly hauled it in, Jake would take it off the line, throw it back and say, "Nobody catches a fish on this boat before the captain!"

ALL THE HOMES AT THE BEACH were in constant need of maintenance. Situated on the shores of the Delaware Bay, they were subjected to par-

A classic Gandy's Beach fixer-upper/ handyman special.

ticularly harsh elements: bitter cold in the winter, baking sun in the summer, corrosion from saltwater, and wind, always lots of wind.

Contractors were seldom called upon as most folks there were do-it-yourself-ers. As soon as a project was under way, neighbors would appear like ants at a picnic. Expert advice was freely handed out, but someone who actually knew what they were doing would pitch in, and some might even scrounge up left-over materials from some other fix.

Projects were evaluated by how many beers it took to accomplish them. A simple window repair might only be a two-beer job. Plumbing was usually much more involved and could be anywhere from 3 beers to several cases, according to how many advisors and/or workers were involved.

At some point, the stairs to Painter John's upstairs deck had rotted out and needed to be replaced, so Jake, Irv, and Trader Joe (another neighbor) became deeply involved. Irv at one point produced a level. Jake told him to put the level away or he and Trader Joe were quittin'. Irv tried to explain that with stairs, you had to use a level, to which Jake replied, explaining the simple physics of beach engineering, "Irv, if it looks level…it's level!"

PAINTER JOHN WAS ONCE trying to remove the old cast iron waste pipe under his house so that he could replace it with PVC. He worked on it for three hours and was making no progress other than wearing out hacksaw blades. While this was happening, Jake and Joe arrived and sat assessing the situation for a while. Jake, being an astute individual, could see exactly what was going on, but nonetheless asked John what he was trying to do. Painter, obviously frustrated, explained that he was trying to get the damn pipe off. Jake said, "Get me a hammer." Painter was befuddled and said, "You can't do nothin' with a hammer." Jake just said "Get me the hammer." Now armed with a hammer, Jake approached the stubborn pipe, studied it for a moment, and gave it one smart whack, whereupon the pipe disintegrated.

WE HAD A COMBINATION radio/cassette player in our house at Gandy's. It was our only source of manufactured entertainment. Radio reception was not good, however, except for the local station that emanated from Bridgeton, NJ: WSNJ. The programming seemed as if it was broadcast from a time capsule, and it very nearly was. The studio, located in a farm field outside of Bridgeton, was equipped with microphones from the 1940s. They had no computers, just a typewriter. In 1994, they were forced off the air for more than three weeks when an ice storm damaged their broadcasting antenna.

Originating in 1937, WSNJ was the voice of the Bayshore.

The station specialized in community affairs, providing a daily lineup of school lunch menus, farm reports, and pet advice. It broadcasted local football and basketball games; The Polka Show was featured on Saturday afternoons, hosted by Polka Tom. The immensely popular Old Country Store served as a call-in classified outlet offering tractors, furniture, used clothing, potential yard sale items, and, on one occasion, a cow.

I recall a memorable moment listening to another favorite, the Lost & Found Show, when a gentleman called in to ask if anyone had found the five hundred dollars he left at a bus stop in downtown Bridgeton.

Naturalist Don Murray hosted a nature program that welcomed questions from listeners. One desperate caller wanted to know how to get rid of a bee's nest. Don responded, "I know how to get rid of it but I can't tell you." Another caller who wanted to hunt mud hens needed advice on how to attract them. (Click two stones together). Somehow this led back to the topic of bee removal again, but Don insisted he couldn't reveal the process. He then offered advice on natural remedies: if you were ever out in the woods and you came down with a headache, break a branch off of a willow tree and chew on it, it would ease the pain. And he was right. Long ago, the original population, (who knew a thing or two about holistic medicine) discovered the pain-reducing properties of willow bark. It contains salicin, a compound similar to aspirin.

Finally, as he was about to sign off, the bees were brought up one last time and he announced "I'm not supposed to tell you this, but here's how to get rid of the bees. Get some gasoline, mix it with some oil, spray it on the bee's nest and light it on fire."

Nearly all the advertising on WSNJ was for local businesses. The announcer for many of the commercials was the station's go-to guy, George Moore. He could be heard crooning: "It's a beautiful day on the Delaware Bay, with Shirley and the crew," or, "The crabs are here", in a sing-song whisper plugging Dill's Seafood. George was the station's sports announcer as well, covering the Bridgeton Invitational Baseball Tournament each summer. He also hosted an occasional live show on Friday evenings that was broadcast remotely from the Charlesworth Hotel in Fortescue. The Sportsman's Hotline featured fishing reports and tall tales from the week's adventures on the Bay. During breaks, the audience would gaze dreamily out of the picture windows watching the sun go down over the Delaware Bay while being entertained by the accordion stylings of Francoise.

The Charlesworth is a landmark that has existed in Fortescue in one form or another since 1925. It was built by Ruella Charlesworth, a businesswoman from Bridgeton, as a ten-room hotel with a bakery in the basement. A spartan retreat, it lacked indoor plumbing and featured only cots for sleeping in rooms that were more like cubicles. A restaurant was added later. After the death of Charlesworth, new management changed the name to the Johnson House, but a short time later, it was changed again, this time to the Preston House.

Picturesqe dining at the Charlesworth Hotel

After a devastating flood in 1950, it was acquired by new owners who revived the original name. They, too, had to deal with more of Mother Nature's wrath in 1980 but were able to survive and repair the damage.

The Charlesworth was one of the few restaurants along the bayshore, a region nearly devoid of eating establishments. It could not compete with new-age cuisine of the time and didn't try to, featuring instead an old-fashioned regional seafood menu that also included steaks and some pasta dishes.

But the major appeal was the view provided in the dining room with its floor-to-ceiling windows overlooking the Delaware Bay. There was not a bad seat in the house. The bay could be dark and moody one evening but display one of the most spectacular sunsets to be seen anywhere on the next.

THERE WAS ANOTHER restaurant that we occasioned called the Newport House, situated at the dead-end of a short road through the fields of a local farm. The one-story building looked like a migrant worker's shack tucked in among a grove of red cedar trees. In fact, it had been a migrant worker's shack. It reminded me of Trader Vic's, the famous Polynesian style restaurant chain featuring shabby chic decor loaded with found objects. Vic Bergeron, the visionary and owner of the eateries once found an old tin-roofed garage in San Francisco in the 1950s that he planned on turning into his newest establishment. He gave explicit instructions to the architect hired to do the work: "When you get through turning this into a restaurant I still want it to look like a shed."

The Newport House did not feature Polynesian fare but had the same type of eclectic ambiance, complete with a tin roof, yet it was not in the least bit contrived. An older gentleman we knew only as Don was the owner. He conveniently provided a history of the place on the back of the menu, describing how he and his partner had opened it as a pizza shop and how they took a chance on expanding into a true restaurant.

It was quirky. As you entered, there was a small reception area that featured trays of gaudy costume jewelry for sale. For lighting in the dining room, Don hung industrial size empty mayonnaise jars from the ceiling fitted with light bulbs. You could feel the floor sagging in a few spots in the dining room. There was one restroom for all in the era before unisex, and it housed the water heater, situated so close to the toilet that care had to be taken not to sear your arms or legs or anything else on it. There was no air conditioning, but lovely views of a serene meadow with occasional visits from deer made up for the lack of comfort.

It was a BYOB featuring a basic steakhouse menu that included king crab legs, pasta dishes, and usually a special or two. We thoroughly enjoyed the place and always left feeling stuffed and happy.

The eclectic little restaurant in the woods, the Newport House

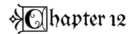

Chapter 12

THE ITALIAN WEDGE

istoric wit Oscar Wilde's opinion of fashion was this: "Fashion is a form of ugliness so intolerable that we have to alter it every six months."

He seems to have been quite a natty dresser in his own right, so the quote may have referenced a slavish weakness for trendy rigs. As a well-established playwright, he no doubt felt an obligation toward flamboyance.

There are many among us who are not involved in the theater or any other aspect of show business who would just like to appear reasonably well dressed. But merely looking like your clothes weren't picked from a dumpster comes with a price, and not just that of the apparel either. This is especially true for women, particularly when it comes to footwear.

A staple of fashion for women is the high-heeled shoe. The basic premise is to elongate the leg and make it appear shaplier, but that's where the price comes in. I seriously doubt there are any women who are willing to claim that wearing high heels for any length of time is comfortable. Not to mention that they're not doing their spines any good at all.

But that is the way of fashion. "It is better to look good than to feel good." (Argentinian actor Fernando Llamas, impersonated by Billy Crystal on Saturday Night Live in the mid-1980s.)

You're probably wondering where the wedge connection to this chapter is going to seep in. Well, here we go.

Salvatore Ferragamo who was born in Bonito, Italy in 1898. The eleventh of fourteen children, he made his first pair of shoes for himself at age nine. They were high heels, which had immediate appeal to his sisters who began clamoring for their brother to make shoes for them as well. His fate was sealed at this tender age; he knew what he was destined to do.

After a year of studying shoemaking in Naples he opened a small store in his parent's home. But in 1914, at the age of sixteen, he emigrated to Boston to join one of his brothers, who worked in a western boot factory. After a brief stint making cowboy footwear, he convinced his brothers to move to Santa Barbara, California where they opened a boot shop. Four years later, Ferragamo moved to Hollywood, and opened another boot shop that also specialized in custom made shoes and repairs. He was in the right place at the right time and found himself creating shoes specifically for use in the movie industry.

One of Ferragamo's earliest patents for a wedge shoe was the Zeppa3 from 1937.

But his creations were strictly for visual effect and were not intended for the consumer market. Ferragamo wanted to make shoes for practical use, so he studied anatomy at the University of Southern California.

In 1927, he returned to Italy and opened a shop in Florence on the artsy Via Mannelli. He began doing more serious experimentation with design which led to his patented steel shank in 1931. It was a light metal support for the arch of the foot. But as World War II approached, steel became harder to come by. Out of necessity came another sparkling example of the use of the wedge: He started experimenting with different materials that were cheaper and easier to find, in particular, Sardinian cork. In 1938, Ferragamo created the wedge heel, made entirely of cork, creating a one-piece platform for the foot. He described the inspired process: "pushing and gluing and fixing and trimming until the entire

In 1947, Ferragamo won the Neiman Marcus Award, considered the Oscar of fashion, for this "invisible sandal" which features a wedge heel.

space between the sole and the heel was blocked solid." Success saw the opening of new shops in London and Rome.

In 1951, Ferragamo held his first Italian fashion show in Florence, showing off ever-more innovative designs. Three years later, he introduced what would become an iconic style: a suede ballerina shoe with a strap, originally made for Audrey Hepburn. Not content with footwear, he began designing silk scarves, bags, and introduced a line of off-the-rack clothing created by his daughter Giovanna Gentile Ferragamo.

Salvatore Ferragamo's sense of design and innovation attracted celebrity clients like Eva Peron, the Duchess of Windsor, Marilyn Monroe, Bette Davis, Marlene Dietrich…a nearly endless list.

Ferragamo holds 369 patents pertaining to shoe structure, design, and much more. He died in 1960, but his wife Wanda took over the business, creating the Ferragamo brand that continued to not only break new ground, but attract celebrity clientele like Brigitte Bardot, for whom they designed a velvet ankle boot in 1966. The following year, Ferragamo's son Fiammi Di Dan Guiliano, received the Neiman Marcus Award, twenty years after his father had received the same honor. In 1995, the Salvatore Ferragamo Museum was opened, spotlighting his many contributions to the fashion world.

Today, the Ferragamo brand continues as an international fashion conglomerate dealing in luxury shoes (what else?) for women and men, bags, accessories, watches, perfumes, and eyewear. Wedge shoes still exist of course, along with traditional high heels, but offer better arch support and are a bit easier to maneuver in, preventing nasty spills. The wedge proves worthy once more.

"The Rainbow", designed for Judy Garland in 1938, was a tribute to her performance in the 1939 film, The Wizard of Oz. The shoe is still in production, but obviously with entirely different connotations.

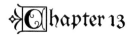

Chapter 13

THE ROAD TO MONEY ISLAND

For an occasional change of pace at Gandy's, we might take a car ride to Money Island to see what was going on there, which was usually nothing. As far as anyone could tell, there was no money at Money Island. An old tale implies Black Beard burying treasure there, but just about every coastal community from the Bahamas to Maine features the same story.

Money Island is similar to Gandy's Beach in that they both came into existence in the late 1930s. But while property at Gandy's was sold as individual lots, Money Island settlers ignored the use of permits, surveys, or licenses, which led to regulatory compliance problems further down the road. Still, it is New Jersey's second most fruitful seafood landing port, unloading in the neighborhood of around twenty million dollars' worth of oysters, blue crabs, menhaden, conch, eels, and horseshoe crabs annually. Unfortunately, the money doesn't stay there.

Money Island is just a stone's throw from Gandy's. To walk directly there would take about five minutes. But due to the nature of the terrain, a paved road is much more convenient, although that requires a trip of about a mile and a half. I used to walk that road every morning for exercise and it was very pleasant except for vicious and unprovoked attacks by bloodsucking insects. At times, the greenheads and deer flies were so profusive that when I returned home, I would feel like I needed a transfusion. But I saw things that would be completely unnoticed whizzing by in a car.

On one particular walk, I came upon a small pile of rust in the middle of the road; it meant something but I wasn't sure what. Further along was another pile of rust, this one a little larger. Evidence was mounting. The next pile contained a rusted O-ring. It was clear someone was about to lose something from their vehicle. By the time I had reached the marina at Money Island and my turn-around point, there it was: a muffler laying in the middle of the road. I had no idea who it belonged to, but everyone else within ear-shot would find out soon enough.

THE FOLKS WHO OWNED the Money Island Marina had a young, energetic, Labrador Retriever. One morning's walk, I was about to turn around at the marina and head back to Gandy's when the dog came bounding out to greet me. It was early in the morning and there was no sign of the owners. They were probably still passed out in their trailer. He was glad to see me and after I fussed all over him, I told him to stay, and tried to continue my walk. But he ignored my commands and decided to accompany me on my walk. So I continued as the dog ran wild circles around me. He was so happy to have companionship.

The road I was walking on was a conduit through wetlands and, since my new friend was a water dog, he could not resist plowing joyfully through the muck and mire. He did this all the way back to Gandy's Beach. A couple of times he disappeared, and I thought, good, he went back to the marina. But then he showed up again, just as excited as ever.

By now, he was totally soaked and covered in mud. When I reached our house, he was still with me and gave no indication that he would go back to his home. I had no intention of walking back to the marina with him. So I opened the door to my 1970 Honda Civic hatchback that had become known as the "tuna can" and he jumped in. (My eldest daughter once paid a visit to us at Gandy's with her boyfriend, and when he saw the Honda he asked, "Does it run?" That was actually a pretty intuitive question. In twenty years that poor car had never had an oil change).

In no time, the interior became smeared with black marsh mud. I drove my filthy new best friend back to the marina, and by now, Gale, his owner was out and about. She yelled at him when he jumped out of the car and I explained how he had followed me on my walk. She didn't bother to thank me for returning him and even gave me the impression that it was somehow my fault that he had followed me. But no good deed goes unpunished, so I returned to our house and guess what I spent the rest of my morning doing?

▶ ▶ ▶

MONEY ISLAND IS LOCATED at the very end of Money Island Road, where it connects with Nantuxent Drive and follows the snake-like contour of Nantuxent Creek until its eventual dead-end. Another unpaved road branches off Nantuxent Drive which is shown on maps as East Nantuxent Drive, but is more familiar to locals as Shell Lane because of its bed of crushed oyster shells. Along its meandering route, Nantuxent Drive crosses over a small inlet where an abandoned oyster boat sat rotting in the mud. Someone had deposited a 350 gallon home heating oil tank on its deck, and I always wondered why: "I gotta get rid of this oil tank. Think I'll put in on that boat." There were a lot of abandoned oyster boats at various locales along the bayshore due to the collapse of the industry in the 1950s. Most of them have long since disintegrated.

One of the boats that unloaded its catch at Money Island belonged to commercial fisherman Robert Munson. He was a fascinating looking gentleman who sported a "lion's mane", that is, the facial hair styling of

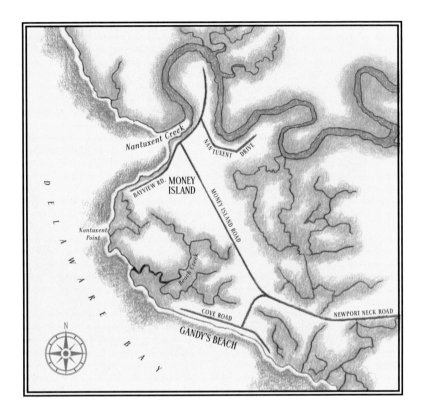

a beard with no mustache, much like the Amish fashion. His was the indelible image of a rugged man of the sea from an earlier time, like the Gloucester fisherman, except this was New Jersey. His specialty was menhaden, also known as bunker, which is why he was called "Bunker Bob" by some, but we always respectfully referred to him simply as Mr. Munson.

His life was as colorful as his appearance. Born in Brooklyn, he served in the US Navy as a submariner during the cold war era, which must have been a nerve-wracking experience, knowing that at any moment he could have been called upon to unleash World War III. After military service, he worked as an Aquatic Consulting Engineer with

United Engineers and Constructors in Philadelphia. Upon retiring, he moved to Newport in Downe Township to establish a Christmas Tree farm and a new career as a bunker fisherman. He also served on the Cumberland County Board of Agriculture and the Fisherman's Council.

Bunker is not a good eating fish, in fact, it's not even a good-looking fish. But a large school of bunker frolicking near the surface of the water can be a giddy distraction as their bodies create a silver froth in the sunlight.

Historically, menhaden has long been an important commercial source for oil, actually outdistancing whale harvests. It's also processed into fish meal, animal feed, a dietary supplement due to its high omega-3 fat content, as fertilizer, and who knows how many other uses. The old school book legend of Squanto teaching the pilgrims to plant a fish with their corn was actually referring to menhaden. But Mr. Munson's catch was sold to commercial crabbers to use for bait. Crabs absolutely adore bunker.

THE MARINA AT MONEY ISLAND had a public boat launch. Some boaters in the region preferred it to the Gandy's Beach marina which had a shallow entrance, making it unusable at low tide.

My friend Harry found this out the hard way on one memorable occasion. He tried to get his sailboat, the *Gumbo Ya Ya*, into the Gandy's marina but his keel plunged into the muddy bottom and he was stuck fast. The incident drew a small but enthusiastic crowd, some of whom jumped into the water to help free the boat, while the remaining onlookers provided advice from the safety of the deck,. During the process of rocking the unfortunate vessel back and forth, a fitting broke, forcing a ride to the hardware store in Cedarville and a near collision with a honey dipper. Eventually the *Gumbo Ya Ya* was freed, given a guest slip, and the repair was made.

Harry's nautical adventures seemed to go from one extreme to the oth-

Despite its backwater persona, Money Island provides a landing for millions
of dollars' worth of seafood every year.

er as exemplified by an earlier effort with another sailboat, the *Dog Star*. It was decided that the Money Island marina would provide plenty of room to maneuver and had deeper water. However, the marina was located at the mouth of Nantuxent Creek, whose currents could be treacherous.

After launching the *Dog Star* with his whole family on board, Harry spent the next two hours fighting the tide, the current, and the fact that water was pouring in due to leaving his plug out, while trying to coax the *Dog Star* out into the Delaware Bay. He never made it out of Nantuxent Creek.

▶ ▶ ▶

WHILE MONEY ISLAND was (and still is) a commercial port, the Money Island Marina catered to sport fishermen and casual boaters. It consisted of a small, weather-beaten cafe/bait shop/fishing supply shack with a large deck in front that stood on the edge of Nantuxent Creek. The building featured a mounted shark on the outside, with weather-worn aqua and royal blue trim. The place was never intended to be a beauty parlor, but if you wanted to describe it more accurately, you might call it "Delaware Bay chic." Roger and Gale acquired it after it sat idle for quite some time, and gradually turned it into party central. There was frequent CB radio banter between the marina and fishermen reporting on the conditions and if and where the fish were biting.

Painter John kept his boat *Stormy* at the Money Island Marina tied to a floating dock that Roger had found somewhere on the cheap. He took me and my son out fishing on a number of occasions and we always had a good time, but my youngest daughter felt left out. One day she sweetly asked "Uncle Paint" if he would take her fishing some time. Painter said regretfully that it just didn't occur to him to take her fishing because, well, she was a girl. But now that she asked, he would be happy to take her.

And so he did. It was late summer and the black flies were in full attack mode, so we outfitted her with long pants and tucked them into her socks; the black flies are notorious ankle biters. They made ready with plenty of bait, soda and snacks, and all the proper gear, and off they went out onto the bay.

They motored out to six buoy and dropped their lines in. Nothing. They tried again and again but the fish were not biting. So Painter decided to try their luck at 32 buoy where he hoped they might catch a shark; he knew kids loved to catch sharks. But this time when they dropped their hooks in, it seemed like the fish were lining up like relatives at a free buffet table, waiting to get caught. Painter laughed that they were practically jumping into the boat.

Before long, had they caught their limit of weakfish–fourteen per person. It was time to head back, so Painter John hailed Roger on the

An early version of the marina at Money Island when it was known
as Pollino's. Drawing courtesy Clayton West.

CB radio and announced they were coming in with a full load. Excited chatter crackled on the radio as other fishermen heard the news. It wasn't every day that a ten-year-old girl, or even an adult, had such a successful outing. They arrived at the Money Island Marina, tied up the boat, and laid out their catch for the day. It was hard to say who was proudest that day: Painter John, my daughter, or me.

One of the admirers of the catch was a regular at the marina known as Jake the Snake. That was his CB handle. Apparently, nobody knew his real name but that was not unusual. People came to the bay not only to fish, but to assume a different life and identity that allowed them to escape their personal rat race, however briefly.

Jake was a relentless presence on Citizen Band, keeping everyone who tuned in informed of where the fish were biting, what kind, who was fishing, and, of course, where he was. His friend Mikey was out one sunny day fishing for croakers. Jake hailed him and asked if he had any extra bait, as he was getting low. Mikey replied sure, he had some, to which Jake responded, "Where are you?" "I'm near Miah Maull", said Mikey (referring to the Miah Maull Lighthouse, a popular fishing spot off Fortescue). "I was just there and I didn't see you," complained Jake. This CB search went on for some time until Mikey finally told Jake, "You see that jet plane flying over?" "Yeah I see it," replied Jake. Mikey shot back, "Well I'm right underneath it."

Later in October, Painter John took my daughter out fishing again along with my wife. This time they were going for stripers. Striped bass is a highly prized game fish, not only in the Delaware Bay but along the entire East Coast and the Gulf of Mexico. They can grow as large as five feet in length and weigh upwards of seventy-five pounds. These are not easy to catch like weakfish. They require different bait as well. Weakfish enjoy shedder crabs, but stripers need more incentive: large chunks of bunker about as big as a man's fist are threaded onto the hook.

More formally known as Morone Saxatilis, *or Striped Bass, the striper can grow up to 59 inches. It is the wet dream of many an Atlantic Coast fisherman.*

Painter John also brought a bucket of chum to try and draw them in close to the boat. Most girls might be repulsed by a bucket of fish guts, but not my daughter. She was actually enjoying shoveling the chum overboard. (To no one's surprise, she is now a gainfully employed Marine Scientist).

The effort paid off. Before long, my daughter hooked something big–really big. Her line played out quickly, making an unmistakable zzzzzz sound, music to a seasoned fisherman's ears. Painter quickly put aside his rod and came to her aid. He showed her the technique for reeling the fish in and helped her get it in the boat: a ten-pound, thirty-six-inch striped bass. They returned to Money Island to show off the catch. She could barely hold it up, complaining that it was heavy, the gills were sharp, and that it was slimy.

She had now become a celebrity; she and her striper were written up as "the catch of the day" in the Delaware Bay Report column of *The Fisherman* magazine.

Roles were reversed that day: while the girls were out fishing, my son and I went to the annual Cranberry Festival in Chatsworth, NJ, wandering aimlessly through the crowds and making snarky comments about the future yard sale items for sale.

▶ ▶ ▶

FOR OUR WEDDING ANNIVERSARY one year, my wife and I jettisoned the kids and were looking forward to spending a quiet weekend at Gandy's and a celebratory dinner at the Newport House. But after settling in for some relaxation, word came through the grapevine that something interesting was going on at Money Island. As very little of anything occurred there, our curiosity was piqued.

We put on our best old clothes and motored over to the Money Island Marina. When we arrived, there was indeed something going on.

THE BOOK OF WEDGES

A small Boston whaler manned by the Coast Guard Auxiliary was just pulling up to the dock with a unique cargo. They were returning from a cruise to the Ship John Shoal Lighthouse located a few miles up the bay at the mouth of the Cohansey River. Onboard were the original wooden molds that had been used to fabricate the wrought-iron superstructure of the light in the mid-1870s. Recently classified as excess by the Federal Government, the lighthouse was being turned over to private ownership, prompting the removal of the molds. They were placed on the dock where the Auxiliary crew and civilians alike, including myself, took advantage of a rare photo opportunity.

There had been many other photo-ops with the lighthouse when it was displayed at the International Centennial Exposition in Fairmount Park in Philadelphia in 1876. The exhibit also featured the lighthouse keeper, who lived on site during the celebration. After the exhibition was over, the lighthouse was transported down the river and placed on a cast iron base in the Delaware Bay. And there is has remained ever since.

(The Ship John Light seems tied to our wedding anniversaries for some unknown reason. One of our previous celebrations was held at the now defunct Ship John Inn in Greenwich which I described in my first book, *The Illustrated Delaware River*. It involved a boat trip to see the Ship John Light in person after dinner.)

After the excitement had diminished and things returned to their usual pace, my wife and I returned to Gandy's and called to make dinner reservations at the Newport House. Much to my horror, I was told they were booked up for the evening. How could that be? They were never booked up! This was a little shack out in the middle of nowhere! Our moods tumbled. Life was supposed to be perfect at the beach; it was created by Divine Providence for celebrations.

Dejected, we sat outside and tried to come up with alternative dining plans. The bay in front of us was choppy and sloshed over the wall.

The Ship John Lighthouse made its first appearance at the International Centennial Exposition at Fairmount Park in Philadelphia in 1876. After the festivities concluded, it was moved to its present location on the Delaware Bay.

Painter John soon emerged from his house and, spotting us sitting next door, he waved and we exchanged greetings. We chatted a bit, telling him about our adventure at Money Island, and how it was our anniversary, and that we wouldn't be able to go to the Newport House as planned. He was quiet for a moment, and then in his inimitable style, announced he would take care of everything and he would cook us an awesome anniversary dinner. We said, no, we couldn't allow him to do that, but he insisted. He took a London Broil steak out of his freezer and placed it outside on his porch railing. I was a little hesitant concerning the outcome, but knowing Painter John, I had the feeling it was not the first time he had done this.

It was a beautiful September day, but slightly windy and chilly. I still had reservations about the condition of a piece of frozen, raw meat thawing at the mercy of the elements. But my fears were unfounded. The combination of wind and sun proved the perfect method for defrosting a steak in record time, and while we chatted and enjoyed a few cocktails, it was soon ready to hit the grill. John was true to his word and prepared an outstanding dinner. The spectacle of the sun setting over the bay before us as we supped was incomparable.

It was the culmination of a perfect day: we encountered a piece of history that very few people ever get to see, had our hopes dashed, then resurrected, enjoyed a lovely dinner with a good friend, and didn't get food poisoning. One of many cherished moments at the beach.

➤ ➤ ➤

ONE BRIGHT, SUNNY AFTERNOON, we road bicycles to Money Island which was thoroughly enjoyable and gave a whole new perspective to visiting a place that we had been to countless times before. I even wrote a song about the experience:

THE ROAD TO MONEY ISLAND

On the road to Money Island,
That's where I fell in love.
On the road to Money Island,
Underneath the sunny skies above.

Didn't know where we were going,
As we pedaled down the thoroughfare.
All the birds were sweetly singing,
And the breeze was blowing through our hair.

(Chorus)
Listen to the music of the fiddler crabs,
Taste the oyster crackers by the bay.
Mister great blue heron doesn't have a care,
The muskrats love to sing and play.

On the road to Money Island,
That's where I long to be.
On the road to Money Island,
With my sweetheart riding there with me.

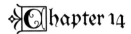# Chapter 14

THE WAY OF THE WEDGE

he only time I can remember working with clay was when I was maybe eight or nine years old, staying overnight with my mother at my aunt and uncle's house on a farm in Southeast Pennsylvania. My uncle had a .22 rifle and he shot it frequently, mostly at birds. As a result, there were many spent shell casings lying around. He never bothered picking them up or his cigarette butts either. I don't want to imply that my relatives were hillbillies…

I've always been a morning person, even at that tender age, and to amuse myself before anyone else was up I would gather the empty .22 shells and then mold new bullets for them out of some modeling clay that my mother bought me. I showed them to my uncle who would grunt something and then go out into the yard and kill a chicken for dinner that night. Those clay bullets were pretty small and uniform so I wouldn't say that there was anything particularly artsy about them.

But there are many talented people who do remarkable things with clay, like making pottery and ceramic pieces, useful and quite beautiful objects that require a good deal of skill to create. To ensure that these products will be the best quality, there is a task that needs to be performed in order for the clay to be at peak usability. And for that, they turn to our old friend, the wedge. Actually, they don't use a literal wedge, but prepare their clay using a process called *wedging*.

Apparently, potters are not fond of this procedure because it takes some time, but it's a necessary evil that needs to be performed to remove air bubbles and hard spots from virgin or recycled clay, and to make it more pliable and uniform. There are even special tables built just for that purpose.

There are several techniques used for wedging: one is the Rams Head in which a lump of clay is pushed with the heels of the hands away from you, then rolled back toward you. The Spiral is similar to the Rams Head but uses a spiral motion. There is the erotic sounding Stack and Slam, and the very sensual Wheel Wedging. Once the clay has been properly manipulated, it's time for the potter to work their particular magic. There are infinite varieties of pottery and ceramics with endless uses.

I've always been drawn for some reason to redware, so named for its distinct reddish tone which can be glazed or not. It was the utilitarian crockery used throughout the colonies of North America. I find it particularly earthy and homey, especially when it's been slip-decorated: an ornamental batter of extra clay is applied to a hard surface by piping it on, like icing on a cake, and then fired. A classic jug is illustrated on the preceding page, but there are dozens of other examples of uses: sugar bowls, platters, teapots, plates, mugs, cups, etc.

➤ ➤ ➤

WE'RE NOT DONE with wedges just yet.

The wedge is formally described as "a piece of hard material with principal faces meeting in a sharply acute angle, for raising, holding, or splitting objects by applying a pounding or driving force, as from a hammer."

It's such a simple object, but its name comes from a surprisingly diverse variety of sources: Old English *wecg*, Proto-Germanic *wagjaz*, Middle Dutch *wegge*, Dutch *wig*, Old High German *weggi*, from a German dialect *Weck*, and aside from the Latin *cuneus*, (mentioned previously), it could refer to a plowshare.

It is one of the earliest and most useful tools in existence. Stone Age people fashioned wedges out of antlers and bone, and we already know about the Ancient Egyptian's fascination with immense stones, which they were able to lift by pounding bronze wedges underneath them.

For those of you who are scientifically inclined, take the length of the sloping side of the wedge and divide it by the length of the thick end of the wedge. Therefore the formula for a wedge is:

The more acute the angle of the wedge, the more mechanical advantage it will have.

THERE ARE FLANGE WEDGES, industrial rubber wedges, wobble wedges (used for stabilizing furniture), shims (which are integral to hanging a door or installing a window), door stops, the pillow wedge, a spot on the Balboa Peninsula in Newport Beach, California, popular with surfers known for its wedge-shaped waves. And even though we don't think of it that way, a nail is a wedge. Unlike a screw, which is a different dynamic altogether, or a bolt that needs a pre-existing hole to work, the nail is forced into wood because of its tapered end.

The wedge can also be a food item. In fact, it is: the Wedge sandwich. Known throughout the country by a variety of names including sub, hero, hoagie, or grinder, the wedge is unique to Westchester County, New York, and Fairfield County, Connecticut. It's an Italian-style sandwich usually comprised of meats, cheeses, and vegetables, but can also apply to other ingredients served on a roll, such as a chicken parm wedge. The origin of the name is hard to pin down. Some believe that a Yonkers deli owner came up with the name, but he was felled by several stray bullets before he could explain the reasoning behind it.

While the Westchester Wedge is clearly a made-to-order comestible, either enjoyed in-house or consumed remotely, it is intended to satisfy. But for those folks on the go who are forced to contend with hunger in a limited time frame, vending machines offer a joyless, mass-produced mealtime solution: an engineered product presented in a hinged, clear plastic, 3.5-inch wedge-shaped container, designed to accommodate a precisely divided sandwich. (Some even offer a Tamper Evident feature). Hideous.

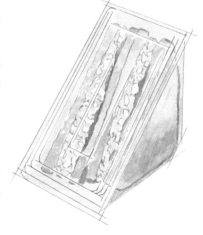

Earlier, also in conjunction with food, we observed how wedges of pie can be used to display data. A slice of cheese is of course a wedge as well, but "cheese chart" doesn't sound right. Pie and cheese wedges both originate from an elliptical shape, (although a whole cheese is referred to as a wheel), but cheese just isn't taken seriously enough to be trusted with important statistics. Cheese is a far more versatile ingredient, however, which is why we rarely hear of baked mac and pie, or pie burger, or pie fondue.

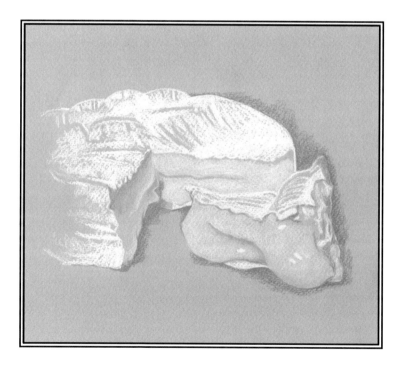

A wedge of good, runny, stinky cheese is not to be taken lightly.

WEDGES ARE USED in a vast variety of ways during ship construction, including shoring up the hull in the building process and dry dock repairs. They are also used in conjunction with an implement known as a "dog". Hundreds of these are used in the construction of metal ships, helping to bend steel plates onto the curved surface of the hull.

Thin, wedge-shaped strips also known as splines are glued into beveled seams between hull planking of wooden ships. These can be used to take the place of traditional caulking in older boats which consisted of hemp fiber soaked in tar known as "oakum."

Notice that the only things keeping this large vessel in an upright position in drydock are of course–wedges.

▶ ▶ ▶

WE NOW FOCUS on the wedge in the abstract, used as the subject of a cliched metaphor, "driving a wedge…" referencing the act of alienating two or more people for personal gain. But it can be expressed in a wide variety of configurations:

COME BETWEEN

as lamented in the old Country & Western song, *"My girlfriend ran off with my best friend, and I sure do miss him."*

DIVIDE

which is what the Delaware River does to the states of Delaware, New Jersey, Pennsylvania, and New York.

STRAIN

expressed by Samuel Johnson: *"Great works are performed not by strength, but perseverance."*

SET AGAINST

explained by Mark Twain, *"Whenever you find yourself on the side of the majority, it is time to pause and reflect."*

IGNITE

just about any conversation involving politics.

TEAR APART

a complete Ambrose Bierce book review:
"The covers of this book are too far apart."

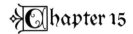

Chapter 15

LIMA BEANS

uring the period we spent at Gandy's, Cumberland County epitomized the old chestnuts "going back in time", and, "where time stands still." The clock did seem to have frozen in the 1950s and refused to advance even a minute. It was an impoverished rural area due mostly to the collapse of the oyster industry, and nothing else had replaced it. The inhabitants were well aware of their plight and kept mostly to themselves.

It seemed as if every property had a couple of old cars in the yard that hadn't been run for years, waiting for a part, and a boat, always a boat. I remember seeing a seventeen-footer that was for sale in front of someone's house. It was painted black with pink lettering that spelled out the name: *No Fat Chicks*. It sat there for a long time.

To a visitor from congested, chaotic suburbia, it seemed charmingly quaint and refreshing. This was the country, with nurseries, and farms, and road side produce stands in front of weathered homes and barns. The offering was much the same at each one: tomatoes, corn, zucchini, peppers, cucumbers, and maybe some eggplant. I recall one stand in front of an elderly gentleman's small farm where he grew an assortment of tomatoes that he labeled Italian tomatoes, cherry tomatoes, and a suspiciously familiar-looking variety of "round tomatoes."

Some of the stands sold flowers too. Mrs. Casper, who had a farm on Newport Neck Road, grew "tuba roses", which are actually "tuberoses." She had bunches of them at the tiny stand in front of her house. They are an incredibly pungent flower, to the point that their aroma could be stifling if they were in a room without good ventilation; even bugs were repelled. For that reason, the windows were always open at our house when they graced our meager table.

There is many a Garden State native who has gone on to great things after growing up on a diet of South Jersey produce.

As a food-loving person, I always enjoyed foraging at the local stands. But the late summer offered a new quest: to find fresh lima beans. Lima beans are one of my favorite vegetables, although some people, like a former friend, describe them as "little sandbags." They are becoming increasingly difficult to find, particularly "pole limas", I suspect because they are too labor-intensive for commercial growers. They are a climbing vegetable and need a trellis to support them, as opposed to "bush limas" that do not.

TRAVELING SOUTH FROM CUMBERLAND COUNTY leads onto the Cape May peninsula, and Cape May County, home to West Cape May, once known as the Lima Bean Capital of the East Coast. To honor that legacy, the city holds a festival every fall that features the little sandbags in a variety of roles: the lima bean queen, the lima bean polka, lima eating contests, and the requisite crafters and vendors. The celebration came about due to the recovery from the great depression in the late 1930s. Farmers in the region found that the lowly lima could be a successful cash crop due to its fondness for the soil. For many years growers in the area had a contract with Hanover Foods in Pennsylvania. As much as 1,000 acres were devoted to limas. West Cape May became a sea of lima beans. But tastes and food trends changed, and the boom times ended, much like the oyster industry in Cumberland County, although more slowly and not as drastically.

Cumberland County Route 553 follows the contour of the Delaware Bay beginning in Cedarville and dead-ends at the Maurice River. It was along this road that many of the produce stands could be found. But lima beans are a different animal; the established stands usually did not have them. They were the lone crop of rugged individuals. Someone may have been secretly growing them in their back yard all year long waiting for this moment, and you had to be ready. A sharp eye was required.

One of my excursions to find the elusive beans took me through the old oyster town of Port Norris. On the main street (which was still Rte. 553), I happened to spot a hand-lettered sign attached to a wooden basket of lima beans in front of a Victorian-era house that announced: "LIMA BEANS-$18.00." I pulled over to the curb and came to a halt next to the sign. I got out and tried to look conspicuous. This was the normal procedure for summoning the proprietor. There was not a steady stream of traffic in Port Norris, so the seller relaxed in his house and peeked out of the window every once in a while to see if there were any customers.

Before long an old man came shuffling out in his stocking feet. We exchanged greetings and, of course, the subject of my stopping: lima beans. I said I wanted to buy a basket. He said he would be right back, he had to go in back of his house to get them. Apparently, the basket by the curb was just for show. He soon returned with another basket of limas and dumprd them into a paper shopping bag.

The lima bean man was talkative, perhaps brought on by some day drinking, judging from the scent, and proceeded to let me in on some hot gossip. It was a known fact that one of the oyster shuckers at the Bivalve Packing Company was having an illicit affair with the plant foreman. If his wife found out there was going to be serious trouble.

Just on the other side of a stretch of marshland from Port Norris is Bivalve, an old fishing village that sits right on the Maurice River, once the epicenter of New Jersey's fabled oyster industry. Although the oyster population had steeply declined, there was still a meager business in oyster processing, particularly at the Bivalve Packing Company. Many of its workers lived in Port Norris, where secrets were hard to keep, apparently. In hushed tones, the lima bean man continued offering more juicy details of the affair as it became apparent that he just couldn't hold it in any longer. I became more and more uncomfortable, concerned that I knew too much already. I wanted to escape lest the trouble should begin while I was there, so I politely interrupted his expose, paid him for the beans, and quickly drove out of Port Norris.

THAT EVENING, we indulged in fried shrimp with cocktail sauce and, of course, lots of delicious, freshly cooked lima beans swimming in butter...with a hint of intrigue.

Chapter 16

THE UNSPEAKABLE WEDGE

Lastly, for those with an underdeveloped sense of humor who have probably been waiting in anticipation, we must unfortunately confront…the wedgie. This predicament, either self-inflicted or the result of a crass prank, does indeed belong in a volume of wedge-related topics. And even though I do have standards, I suppose we're going to have to deal with it.

Legitimate history gives us very little to go on, but the practice was probably introduced around the same time that underwear began to be used. Animal skins are not conducive to the act as they are not supple enough. Cloth, particularly cotton, is better suited for the task, but synthetics can stretch to unimaginable limits.

While wedgies can be uncomfortable (and humiliating), they are usually harmless. But there is one recorded instance of a fifty-year-old man who sustained long-term effects after his thirty-four-year-old wife caught him with his pants down, as it were. For the next six years, he experienced numbness and tingling in his left leg, which eventually went away, especially when his wife stopped giving him wedgies.

There is also the gruesome case of a ten-year-old boy who needed surgery to reattach one of his testicles to his scrotal lining after a particularly brutal wedgie. And one death: an Oklahoma man confessed to police that he had given his stepfather an atomic wedgie, which apparently caused the man to die from asphyxiation.

Since this volume is obviously a work of taste and refinement, I'm not going to wallow anymore in the depths of such a topic.

In fact, that's about all the wedges I have for you at this time. As I wander through the rest of my life, I will no doubt discover, regretfully, more examples that should have been included here, but such is life. By the way, did I tell you that my favorite baseball player of all time is Wedgie Jackson?

This illustration is based on "marginalia", a term used to describe the doodling of playful scribes during the middle ages. Books were expensive hand-written volumes that involved tedious copying, occasionally driving the scribes to distraction. They became notorious for creating cartoon fantasies depicting flatulence, scatological humor, forbidden sex scenes, grotesque monsters, and, for some unexplainable reason, psychotic rabbits with axes. These images could be found in the margins of even the holiest of works. Obviously, the wedgie belongs here.

EPILOGUE

In the introduction to this book, I promised to reveal how Painter John came by that nickname. It goes like this.

Painter John was born John Gilligan. Yes, the same name as the loopy Bob Denver character from the beloved TV series Gilligan's Island. He owned the house next to ours at Gandy's Beach.

During a violent nor'easter in 1980, the first floor of John's house sustained severe damage, so he recruited a friend with advanced construction skills to handle the repair work. It now fell to John to complete the job by painting the place to be ready for the summer. But John had never painted anything before in his life. He bought what he believed to be enough paint for the job; eight gallons. White. And a brush.

He took two weeks' vacation-time from his job to go to the beach, paint the house, and maybe do a little fishing before the rest of his family would join him. This was a time when weakfish were remarkably plentiful in the Delaware Bay. Weakfish is in the drum family, occasionally referred to as sea trout and a good eating fish. They were so abundant that the nearby community of Fortescue called itself "The weakfish capital of the world!"

When John arrived at the beach, the weather was beautiful, the conditions perfect. He was a responsible man, but he was not made of stone; there was no choice but to postpone his painting assignment to take advantage of the situation. The fishing was indeed so good that he fished and he fished, day after day after day, until there was only one day left before his family would arrive. And on that final day, he decided that just one more little bit of fishing in the morning, a couple of hours, would still leave him plenty of time for the chore at hand. But the weak-fish were biting, the sun was shining, and the couple of hours carried long into the afternoon. By the time he returned and cleaned all the fish he'd caught, it was now nearly five o'clock. John took all the cans of paint from the back of his truck and proceeding to gear himself up for the job ahead. It wasn't long before John's neighbor Jake noticed something was up and came over to investigate.

Now Gandy's Beach is a small community, and as such it's difficult to keep one's business to one's self. Whenever repairs had to be made to a property, nobody used a contractor. As soon as a project was underway, a contingent of neighbors would gradually appear, some to offer advice, some to actually pitch in.

Jake asked, "John, what in the hell are you doing?" "Well, Jake," answered John. "The family's coming down tomorrow and I've got to get the inside of the house painted." Jake then questioned, "That's not much time. What are you gonna do?" "I got a brush", replied John. "I'm just gonna open up the cans and start paintin." Jake said, "John, you need a roller. You can't paint the whole inside of the house with a brush!" John said he didn't have a roller, to which Jake replied that he would get him one. He left and returned shortly with a roller and a paint tray and explained the finer points of how to use them.

Nearly everyone at Gandy's had some sort of nickname; some were CB radio handles that became permanent. It meant you were accepted.

Some old-timers had been called by their nicknames for so long that if you addressed them by their real name, no one would know who you were talking about. If you did not already have a nickname then one would be assigned to you. One gentleman who purchased a house at Gandy's didn't seem to have any distinguishing characteristics, he was just the new guy. He was known as "New Guy" for years afterward. Jake was already a nickname so he didn't need any further embellishment.

Back to our story.

Shortly after Jake had set John on the correct path to the job at hand, another neighbor appeared. Known as Trader Joe, since he was in the business of trading horses, he used the same line of questioning, "John, what the hell are you doin'?" "I've got to paint the whole inside of this house, but Jake said I have to do it with a roller, so now I've got that and it's all good," John answered. Trader Joe said, "You need a broomstick so you can reach the high spots." John replied that he had a broom handle but the broom was still attached. Shaking his head, Trader Joe left and returned with the correct implement: a broom handle with threads on one end that would screw into the roller handle.

Feeling confident that he now had all the equipment, supplies, and tools that he needed, John turned on the radio, dialed in the country music station, and turned up the volume to full blast. He drank a couple of beers and started rolling on the paint. After more beer, he grew even more confident and continued painting like there was no tomorrow...literally. He rolled the walls, the ceilings, and the doors, including the handles. He rolled the mullions on the windows. He rolled the windowsills and the molding. He rolled the refrigerator and the light switches. The floor, which was linoleum, took on a unique and new speckled complexion.

He painted until five-o'clock in the morning and then passed out. The entire interior of the house was completely painted. Later in the morning Jake and Trader Joe came by and woke John up for an inspection. They carefully examined his handiwork and looked at each other, then back at the new paint job, then at John. They declared, "It don't look too damn bad. From now on we're gonna call you Painter John!"

The complete catalog of books to date
by Hal Taylor are:

The Illustrated Delaware River:
The History of a Great American River

Before Penn:
An Illustrated History of the Delaware River Colonies,
1609-1682

Artifacts:
An Illustrated Treasury of Delaware Valley History

The Book of Wedges:
Tales from a Beach